THE SWEEP OF HISTORY TOLD IN COLORFUL DETAIL

AVON BOOKS ◆ NEW YORK

STAN MACK'S REAL LIFE AMERICAN REVOLUTION is an original publication of Avon Books. This work has never before appeared in book form.

AVON BOOKS
A division of
The Hearst Corporation
1350 Avenue of the Americas
New York, New York 10019

Library of Congress Cataloging in Publication Data:

Mack, Stanley.
  [Real life American revolution]
  Stan Mack's real life American revolution / written and illustrated by Stan Mack.
    p.   cm.
  1. United States—History—Revolution, 1775-1783—Caricatures and cartoons. 2. American wit and humor, Pictorial. I. Title.
E298.M33   1994   94-17808
973.7'0207—dc20   CIP

First Avon Books Trade Printing: November 1994

AVON TRADEMARK REG. U.S. PAT. OFF. AND IN OTHER COUNTRIES, MARCA REGISTRADA, HECHO EN U.S.A.

Printed in the U.S.A.

OPM 10 9 8 7 6 5 4 3 2 1

Acknowledgments

First, I'd like to thank Ms. "Red" Johnson (wherever she may be), my social studies teacher at Nathan Bishop J.H.S. who, amazingly enough, let me substitute historical political cartoons for the essays the other kids had to turn in.

Special thanks go to Mark Gompertz; Charlotte and Carl Bode; Marv Gettleman; Ron Chernow; Jesse Lemisch; David Highfill; John Douglas; Peter, Ken, and Pearl Mack; Lew Grimes; Lillian and Herman Rabins; John Racanelli; Morris Braverman; Rick Meyerowitz...

...and, most important, for her love, counsel, and support, Janet Bode, to whom I dedicate this book.

Introduction

My first aim with this book was to tell a good story. It's factually and chronologically accurate and includes as many names, ideas, and events as I could get in without slowing down the pace. But, mainly, I tried to capture some of the spirit, excitement, perils, and follies of the Revolutionary Era.

Imagine looking at history through both ends of a telescope. The great events that propel history are seen alongside the everyday stuff that flavors our lives. Taking the long view, you see congress battling over the idea of independence and the fate of the country. Through the close-up lens, you see the faces of individual people, busy living fragments of the larger picture.

Much, of course, has had to be simplified or has ended up on the cutting-room floor. There were many regional conflicts, local rivalries, political animosities, and religious differences that complicated the colonial times and separated the people. And the reader should keep in mind that to generalize is often to exaggerate.

I have used James Otis and Sam Adams in Boston to represent a lot of the discontent, but there were men and women of all backgrounds and classes who contributed to the struggle. One of the issues historians debate is how much of the leadership for radical action came from the wealthier and better educated and how much came from the ordinary people and their own willingness to force change.

As you read through this book, you will come upon a modern character pushing in from the edges of the page. His name is Carl and he looks like this:

One day Carl appeared on my drawing board. I don't know where he came from, but he knew some history and wasn't shy about sharing it. It seemed to me that letting him stay and comment on the story was a good way to bridge the past with the present for the reader.

A few words here about the graphic form of this book. As with both movies and television, the comic strip is rich with storytelling possibilities. But the caricatures and rubbery figures shouldn't mislead the reader about the seriousness of the history. This is not a book of jokes. The humor comes directly from the research. (The rich colonists really did send their clothes to England for cleaning.) By the way, the drawings will not show you exactly how rifles or wagons work. They are cartoons, funny moments meant to be "read" quickly.

Finally, why is the book called "Real Life"? For many years I have written and drawn a comic strip called "Stan Mack's Real Life Funnies" in the New York weekly newspaper _The Village Voice_. I work like a reporter, covering events, interviewing and sketching people, researching and editing stories, and producing a graphic documentary on life in New York. In my comic strip, real people appear in situations that really happened. My strip is funny and sad, political and personal, just like real life and...history.

CONTENTS

1

1761 – 1775

MONARCHY & MOBS

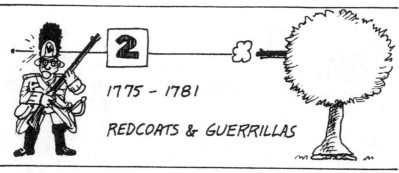

1775 - 1781

REDCOATS & GUERRILLAS

3

1782 - 1789

PROFIT & VIRTUE

1761 - 1775

MONARCHY & MOBS

It's the early 1760s and Britain has finally defeated the French and kicked them out of the New World. The British troops head for home.

Here in America, England's colonies are busily riding a population explosion and business boom.

COLONIAL MERCHANTS AND SHIPBUILDERS ARE RAKING IN BIG PROFITS...

SHOULD WE GIVE OUR WORKERS A RAISE?

NA! THAT'LL SPOIL THEM.

...AND EVERYONE IS BUSY SMUGGLING TO AVOID TRADE RESTRICTIONS IMPOSED BY GREAT BRITAIN.

ROYAL CUSTOMS

ZZZZ

SHHHH

ENGLAND IS HAVING FITS. SHE HAS A HUGE WAR DEBT, SHE CAN'T SQUEEZE ANY MORE TAXES OUT OF HER OWN PEOPLE, AND SHE'S WATCHING SMUGGLERS MAKE A MOCKERY OF HER ATTEMPTS TO REGULATE TRADE THROUGHOUT HER EMPIRE.

THE WHOLE POINT OF HAVING COLONIES IS TO EXPLOIT THEM!

THE COLONIES BLATANTLY IGNORE BRITISH TRADE DUTIES AND SMUGGLE FRENCH SUGAR FOR THEIR LUCRATIVE RUM BUSINESS, PART OF THE INFAMOUS TRIANGULAR TRADE.

HOW THE TRIANGULAR TRADE WORKS

COLONIAL SHIPPERS CARRY SUGAR AND MOLASSES FROM THE WEST INDIES TO NEW ENGLAND WHERE THEY'RE CONVERTED TO RUM. THE RUM IS SHIPPED TO AFRICA...

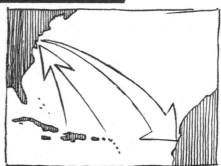

...WHERE AFRICANS, ARABS, AND EUROPEANS HAVE LONG BEEN IN THE SLAVE BUSINESS. THE RUM IS TRADED FOR AFRICANS WHO HAVE BEEN DRAGGED FROM THEIR VILLAGES AND JAMMED ON SHIPS.

THE SHIPS SAIL TO THE WEST INDIES, CENTRAL AND SOUTH AMERICA, AND THE COLONIES. THEY SELL THEIR HUMAN CARGO, LOAD UP ON SUGAR, AND START AGAIN.

FRUSTRATED, ENGLAND TURNS TO **WRITS OF ASSISTANCE**, GENERAL SEARCH WARRANTS THAT ALLOW HER TO BOARD SHIPS SUSPECTED OF SMUGGLING. AND SO:

COLONISTS, LIVING UNDER THE BRITISH MONARCHY, HAD MORE LEGAL RIGHTS THAN MOST PEOPLE IN THE WORLD. IF NOT FOR THESE FREEDOMS, THEY MIGHT NEVER HAVE BEEN ABLE TO REBEL AT ALL.

A QUICK LOOK AT SOME OF THE IMPORTANT PEOPLE AND IDEAS THAT INFLUENCED THE COLONISTS.

NEW ENGLAND PURITANISM

MAN HAS A DUTY TO HIS GOD TO WORK HARD, BE THRIFTY, AND BE UNCOMFORTABLE WITH LUXURY.

MAN WHO TOILS HONESTLY AND PRAISES GOD WILL PROSPER AND FIND SALVATION.

GOD SAYS IF I WORK HARD, I'LL PROSPER. BUT IF I PROSPER, I'LL GET RICH. AND RICHES ARE <u>DECADENT</u>.

THE ENLIGHTENMENT

JOHN LOCKE 1632-1704 ENGLISH INTELLECTUAL

SOCIETY IS AN AGREEMENT AMONG MEN AIMED AT PROTECTING SELF-INTEREST AND INDIVIDUAL FREEDOMS.

REBELLION IS PROPER TO PROTECT LIBERTY AND PROPERTY. (THIS ONLY APPLIES TO THE ARISTOCRACY. THE LOWER CLASSES SHOULD BE TRAINED AS SERVANTS.)

JEAN JACQUES ROUSSEAU 1712-1778
FRENCH PHILOSOPHER

GO TO NATURE AND THERE WORSHIP THE NOBLE SAVAGE.

ALL MEN IN NATURE ARE EQUAL. IT IS CIVILIZATION THAT BRINGS GOOD AND EVIL.

SIR ISAAC NEWTON 1642-1727
ENGLISH SCIENTIST

OUR WORLD IS A WATCH AND GOD IS THE WATCHMAKER.

THE UNIVERSE IS GUIDED BY SCIENTIFIC PRINCIPLES, AND IT IS MAN'S DUTY TO LEARN ITS SECRETS. FOR EXAMPLE, WHY DOES AN APPLE FALL?

GRAVITY WAS A HARD IDEA TO GRASP IN THOSE DAYS.

IN 1761, A TRIAL IS HELD BEFORE THE MASSACHUSETTS SUPREME COURT. THE LAWYER FOR THE MERCHANTS IS BRILLIANT, ERRATIC, MAGNETIC JAMES OTIS. (JAMES ALSO HATES THE BOSTON ELITE BECAUSE THEY SLIGHTED HIS LAWYER FATHER.)

JAMES OTIS

THE LAWYER FOR THE CROWN SAYS THE EXPECTED:

THE WRITS ARE NECESSARY BECAUSE...

... COLLECTING TAXES IS MORE IMPORTANT THAN ANYONE'S RIGHTS.

THEN OTIS MAKES HIS REBUTTAL. HE USES IDEAS LIFTED FROM THE PHILOSOPHICAL THEORIES OF THE DAY.

9

THE CASE IS SETTLED IN FAVOR OF THE CROWN, OF COURSE. BUT THERE ARE MEN WHO HEAR OTIS' WORDS THAT DAY...

SHOCKING! CRAZY! SCARY!

...TOUGH, UPWARDLY MOBIL YOUNG MEN WHO ALREADY THINK THAT ENGLAND AND THE COLONIAL RULING CLASS...

ON THE OTHER HAND...

...ARE OBSTACLES TO THEIR OWN AMBITIONS.

...MAYBE THEY ARE A WEAPON!

BUT IF THESE MEN ARE TO USE IDEAS AS SWORDS TO CHALLENGE ENGLAND, WILL ANYONE FOLLOW THEM?

NATURAL RIGHTS

OVER IN ENGLAND, CHUBBY, INFLEXIBLE 25-YEAR-OLD GEORGE III HAS RECENTLY BECOME KING. NOW HE HAS TO PROVE HE CAN RUN AN EMPIRE.

I AM STRONG, RESOLUTE, KINGLY.

SO SHOW ME AGAIN WHERE THE NEW WORLD IS.

GEORGE III HAS ONLY ONE INTEREST IN THE COLONIES.

YOUR MAJESTY, OUR AGENTS REPORT THAT THE COLONISTS ARE SELFISH CHILDREN WHO CHEAT US.

THOSE INGRATES ARE PART OF THE GREAT BRITISH EMPIRE AND WILL HAVE TO BE TAUGHT A LESSON!

THE COLONIES IN 1763

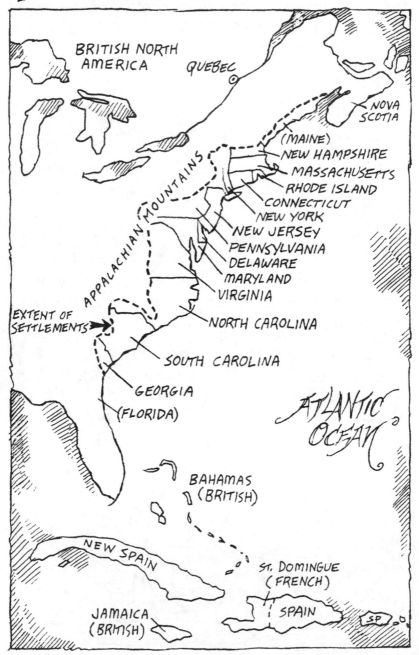

BRITISH NORTH AMERICA

QUEBEC

NOVA SCOTIA

(MAINE)
NEW HAMPSHIRE
MASSACHUSETTS
RHODE ISLAND
CONNECTICUT
NEW YORK
NEW JERSEY
PENNSYLVANIA
DELAWARE
MARYLAND
VIRGINIA
NORTH CAROLINA
SOUTH CAROLINA
GEORGIA
(FLORIDA)

APPALACHIAN MOUNTAINS

EXTENT OF SETTLEMENTS

ATLANTIC OCEAN

BAHAMAS (BRITISH)

NEW SPAIN

St. DOMINGUE (FRENCH)

SPAIN

SP

JAMAICA (BRITISH)

THE COLONIES

To GREAT BRITAIN, THE COLONIES ARE HER PERSONAL THIRD WORLD COUNTRY— A CHEAP SOURCE OF RAW MATERIALS, A MARKET FOR HER GOODS, AND A PLACE TO DUMP UNDESIRABLES...

To PEASANTS AROUND THE WORLD, LEADING WRETCHED LIVES UNDER TYRANNICAL MONARCHIES, THE COLONIES SOUND LIKE THE PROMISED LAND.

STANISLAW, IN AMERICA EVERYONE BECOMES RICH AND RESPECTABLE. GIVE ME ALL YOUR MONEY AND I'LL GET YOU ON A SHIP.

TOO CROWDED TO =OOF= SIT DOWN...

WORMY WATER AND HALF A RAT =SOB= FOR DINNER.

13

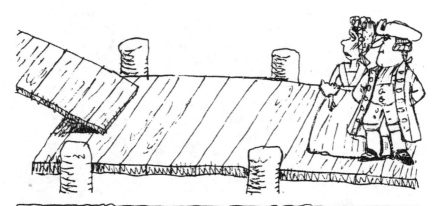

14

THERE ISN'T ANY OFFICIAL NOBILITY BUT THERE ARE THE NEW ARISTOCRATS: THE MERCHANT PRINCES, LAND SPECULATORS, POWER BROKERS...

SEND MY SUIT TO ENGLAND FOR CLEANING. TELL THEM...

..., I MUST HAVE IT BACK IN THREE MONTHS.

DOWN SOUTH THE HAUGHTY PLANTATION OWNERS HUNT FOXES, BREED HORSES, GAMBLE, PARTY, AND PONDER THE GREAT PHILOSOPHERS.

WE'LL CATCH A FOX PUT HIM IN A BOX

THEY STUDY WAYS TO KEEP THEIR SLAVES SUBJUGATED. THEIR LIFESTYLE DEPENDS ON IT.

WE MUST GET POOR WHITE PEOPLE TO FEEL SUPERIOR TO, AND FEAR, SLAVES.

THE ORDINARY PEOPLE ARE TREATED AS CHILDREN BY THOSE IN AUTHORITY WHO CONTROL THE PRICES, PRODUCTION, AND DISTRIBUTION OF GOODS.

HE SHOULD BE DOFFING HIS HAT TO US!

APPLES FOR SALE

BUT, WHILE THE RICH RUN EVERYTHING, ALL THE COLONISTS HAVE BEEN ARGUMENTATIVE AND LITIGIOUS FROM THE START: NORTH AGAINST SOUTH, FRONTIER AGAINST SEACOAST, BIG COLONY AGAINST SMALL.

SEE THAT BLUEBIRD? IT'S THE BOUNDARY OF MY LAND! SO GET OFF!

MY LAND RUNS TO THE PACIFIC AND YOU'RE STANDING ON IT!

PEOPLE JAM THE COURTS, SUING OVER EVERYTHING. AND THEIR LAWYERS, "THE DEVIL'S ADVOCATES," GROW RICH.

17

Among the masses there's a popular tradition of RIOTING. People take to the street in anger over injustices like high prices and food shortages.

There are three injustices that few colonists protest: their own treatment of slaves as chattel, Native Americans as savages, and women as inferiors.

COLONIAL WOMEN ARE NO BASHFUL LAMBS. THEY LEAD PROTESTS, SMOKE AND SWEAR, AND, WHEN THEIR MEN DIE, RUN SHOPS, SHIPS, TAVERNS, AND FARMS...

...WHILE TEACHING SCHOOL AND RAISING FLOCKS OF KIDS. BUT WOMEN HAVE FEW LEGAL RIGHTS. AND THEY OFTEN DIE IN CHILDBIRTH.

NOT THAT ANY SICK PERSON HAS MUCH CHANCE OF SURVIVING THE MEDICAL CARE OF THE DAY.

I PRESCRIBE BLEEDING, PURGING, AND COW DUNG POULTICES.

BY THIS TIME, **SLAVES** HAVE BECOME AN ESSENTIAL PART OF THE SOUTHERN ECONOMY. THEY ARE THE WORK ANIMALS NEEDED TO KEEP UP THE HUGE PLANTATIONS.

PERSONALLY, WE'RE AGAINST SLAVERY, BUT YOU CAN'T LIVE IN VIRGINIA WITHOUT THEM.

AS THE AFRICANS RECOVER FROM THE HORRORS OF THEIR KIDNAPPING, THEY CALCULATE WAYS TO GET FREE OF THEIR TORMENTORS.

INDIGENOUS PEOPLES LIVED ON THIS CONTINENT FOR CENTURIES BEFORE THE EUROPEANS ARRIVED.

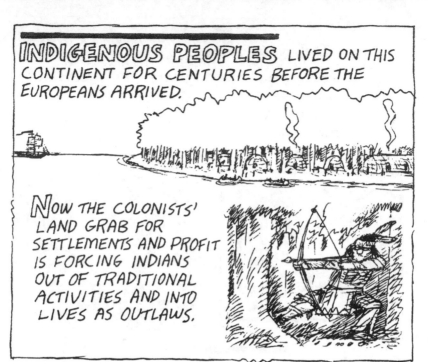

Now THE COLONISTS' LAND GRAB FOR SETTLEMENTS AND PROFIT IS FORCING INDIANS OUT OF TRADITIONAL ACTIVITIES AND INTO LIVES AS OUTLAWS.

And WHEN THE TROUBLE STARTS, IT'LL BE THE CITY LABORERS, WHOSE INCOMES ARE DEPENDENT ON THE RICH MERCHANTS, WHO FIRST UNITE IN ANGER AGAINST <u>ENGLAND</u>.

THE SUGAR ACT

GEORGE III HIRES A MYOPIC NUMBER CRUNCHER, GEORGE GRENVILLE, AS HIS PRIME MINISTER. GRENVILLE LOOKS AT THE BOOKS AND IS HORRIFIED.

WE FIGHT WARS AND SPEND MONEY TO PROTECT THESE BUMPKINS, AND THIS IS HOW THEY REPAY US! IT'S TIME TO REFORM THIS SLOPPY SYSTEM.

ROYAL DEBT

COLONIAL ACCOUNTS RECEIVABLE

GRENVILLE CLOSES THE WESTERN LANDS. HE WANTS TO KEEP HIS TAX PAYERS CLOSE AT HAND AND AWAY FROM TROUBLE WITH THE INDIANS.

CLOSED TO SETTLERS
King George

NOT THAT THAT WILL STOP THE RICH LAND DEVELOPERS LIKE BEN FRANKLIN AND GEORGE WASHINGTON.

THESE BEADS FOR THOSE MOUNTAINS.

I THOUGHT LAND BELONGS TO EVERYBODY.

IN 1764, GRENVILLE PUTS TEETH INTO THE TRADE LAWS ON SUGAR BROUGHT IN FROM THE FRENCH WEST INDIES.

THEN GRENVILLE PULLS SOMETHING NEW. BEFORE, BRITISH CUSTOMS DUTIES WERE USED TO DIRECT TRADE AROUND THE EMPIRE. **BUT**, NOW...➡

➤ ...GRENVILLE STARTS TAXING CERTAIN COLONIAL IMPORTS SPECIFICALLY TO MAKE A PROFIT FOR ENGLAND.

THE MERCHANTS, USED TO HAVING THINGS THEIR OWN WAY, ARE NOT HAPPY. THEY START PAYING ATTENTION TO JAMES OTIS AND HIS IDEAS.

HERE WE INTRODUCE THE MAN WHO REALLY GOT THE WHEELS OF REVOLUTION TURNING, SAM ADAMS OF BOSTON. SAM IS A DOWN-AT-THE-HEELS POLITICIAN, HARVARD GRADUATE, TRUE PURITAN, ENEMY OF THE ELITE, AND AN **ACE AGITATOR** !

THE POOR ARE GOOD, THE RICH ARE EVIL.

SAM ADAMS

NEW ENGLAND WORKERS HAVE ALWAYS GATHERED TOGETHER TO ARGUE POLITICS, AND SAM HAS A CLOSE RELATIONSHIP WITH BOSTON'S LABORING CLASS.

INN

SAM, COME HAVE A TANKARD.

AS SOON AS I GET BACK FROM CHURCH.

SAM SPENDS A LOT OF TIME LISTENING TO THE COMPLAINTS OF DOCKWORKERS, CRAFTSMEN, AND LABORERS.

MY BOSS WEARS SILK SHIRTS AND VELVET SUITS, AND PAYS ME PENNIES !

INN

More and more of the money in the colonies has been ending up in the hands of the wealthy. Sam puts the workers' frustration into words.

THE RICH HAVE STRAYED FROM THE PATHS OF VIRTUE AND ARE KEEPING THE GOODIES FOR THEMSELVES.

FOR AN EDUCATED MAN, SAM, YOU'RE PRETTY SMART.

As Grenville's taxes squeeze the merchants, the merchants squeeze their workers. Soon both are complaining loudly!

I HAVE A RIGHT TO MAKE A PROFIT!

I HAVE A RIGHT TO FAIR WAGES!

The co-instigators, James Otis and Sam Adams, use this discontent to launch a political movement.

IT IS TYRANNY TO TAX PEOPLE NOT REPRESENTED IN PARLIAMENT!

THE COMMON MAN HAS GOD-GIVEN RIGHTS.

OTIS WRITES LETTERS OF PROTEST THAT ARE CIRCULATED TO OTHER COLONIES.

IT'S A WASTE OF TIME. THE OTHER COLONIES ARE ALL CRAZY.

SURPRISINGLY, THE COLONIES RESPOND.

LETTERS FROM NEW JERSEY, MARYLAND, VIRGINIA... THEY AGREE WITH US...

MAIL

THE "BETTER PEOPLE" OF BOSTON ARE NOT AMUSED.

ADAMS AND OTIS ARE JUST ENCOURAGING THE RIFF-RAFF.

ATTACKING THE CROWN IS TREASON!

OTIS IS MAD!

ACTUALLY, OTIS DISCOVERS THAT BEING ACCUSED OF TREASON IS GOOD FOR BUSINESS.

J. OTIS ATTORNEY AT LAW

OPEN

OTIS PROBABLY WAS SLIGHTLY MAD. BY THE LATE 1760's, MENTAL ILLNESS DROVE HIM OUT OF THE STRUGGLE.

IN ENGLAND, GRENVILLE HAS AN ANSWER FOR COLONIAL GRUMBLINGS ABOUT RIGHTS AND TAXATION.

HEY, MOST ENGLISH PEOPLE CAN'T PASS THE PROPERTY REQUIREMENTS FOR VOTING, EITHER...

...BUT WE TAX THEM ANYWAY BECAUSE THEY ARE "IN EFFECT" REPRESENTED IN PARLIAMENT.

THE COLONISTS ARE "IN EFFECT" REPRESENTED IN THE SAME WAY.

ENGLAND, 3630 MILES AWAY BY SEA

A POSTWAR RECESSION HAS HIT THE COLONIES, AND OTIS AND ADAMS ARE LEARNING THAT IDEAS ARE IMPORTANT BUT JOBLESSNESS IS WHAT CREATES SUPPORT FOR RADICAL ACTION.

NATURAL RIGHTS ... AND JOBS... FOR EVERYONE!

NO HELP WANTED

WE'RE WITH YOU!

AS DISCONTENTED WORKERS RALLY TO SAM'S SIDE, GRENVILLE COMES UP WITH A FABULOUSLY STUPID IDEA.

HEH HEH

Stamp Act

THE COLONIES MUST BUY SPECIAL STAMPED PAPER FROM ENGLAND. THE PAPER WILL BE USED FOR:

LEGAL DOCUMENTS, BUSINESS PAPERS, SHIPPING ORDERS, BIRTH CERTIFICATES, LICENSES, ANNOUNCEMENTS, PAMPHLETS, NEWSPAPERS...

THE STAMP ACT

WILL GO INTO EFFECT IN THE FALL OF *1765*, AND VIOLATORS WILL BE TRIED IN THE NEW WAY.

BUT GRENVILLE HAS OVERLOOKED SOMETHING. WITH THIS ACTION HE'S GOING AFTER THE LAWYERS, SHIPOWNERS, PUBLISHERS, DOCTORS, AND CLERGY— THE ONES WITH MONEY, EDUCATION, AND **CLOUT!**

GRRR   GRRR   GRRR   GRRR   GRR O

WITH THE STAMP ACT AS A CATALYST, ENGLAND'S AMERICAN COLONIES BEGIN TO UNITE IN ANGER.

UN ENGLAND, SOME PEOPLE DEFEND THE PROTESTORS. ONE POLITICIAN CALLS THEM, "SONS OF LIBERTY." SAM ADAMS AND HIS BAND OF AGITATORS LOVE IT!

NOW, IN BOSTON, SAM ADAMS AND THE **SONS OF LIBERTY** LEAD THE PEOPLE INTO THE **STREET**!

IN THE FRONT RANKS OF THE DEMONSTRATORS ARE THE TOUGH COLONIAL SAILORS. THEY'VE SUFFERED GREATLY AT THE HANDS OF THE ROYAL NAVY.

THE FIRST ACT IN SAM ADAMS' STREET THEATER IS TO HANG BOSTON'S NEWLY APPOINTED STAMP COLLECTOR, ANDREW OLIVER, IN EFFIGY FROM AN ELM TREE.

SOON THERE WOULD BE "LIBERTY TREES" AND "LIBERTY POLES" IN EVERY TOWN.

SOME OF THE CROWD FOLLOW UP BY TRASHING OLIVER'S HOME. OLIVER, BROTHER-IN-LAW OF LIEUTENANT GOVERNOR THOMAS HUTCHINSON, DECIDES TO RESIGN.

OKAY, I QUIT!

HEY, THIS RIOTING STUFF WORKS!

TWO DAYS LATER, THE MOB CONTINUES ITS RAMPAGE BY WRECKING HUTCHINSON'S MANSION. HUTCHINSON HAS TO GRAB HIS FAMILY AND RUN.

THE AUTHORITIES ARE SHOCKED BY THIS CIVIL DISOBEDIENCE. THEY KNOW WHERE TO LAY THE BLAME.

IT'S THAT RABBLE-ROUSING SAM ADAMS AND HIS CROWD SPOUTING THEIR PATRIOTIC FOOLISHNESS!

POISONING THE MINDS OF THE LOWER CLASSES WITH SUBVERSIVE NONSENSE!

THE MOB GETS AWAY WITH IT BECAUSE THE PEOPLE WON'T IDENTIFY THE GUILTY. OTIS AND ADAMS CONDEMN IT.

DISGRACEFUL!

SHOCKING!

DRAWING ON TRADITIONS OF ASSEMBLING FOR FESTIVALS AND PROTESTS, PEOPLE IN OTHER TOWNS AND VILLAGES QUICKLY BAND TOGETHER.

IT WORKED IN BOSTON, IT CAN WORK HERE.

WE'LL PUT A STOP TO THESE STAMP COLLECTORS.

THESE LOCAL SONS OF LIBERTY GROUPS PUT ON MASKS, PAINT THEIR FACES AND TAKE **ACTION!**

WITH PAINT ON, NO ONE WILL KNOW WHO WE ARE.

TAKE YOUR CHOICE: HANGING IN EFFIGY, TAR AND FEATHERS, HOUSE SACKING, COACH BURNING...

NOW, LOOK! I TOLD YOU NOT TO ACCEPT THAT STAMP COLLECTOR'S JOB.

By October, 1765, people are calling for mass boycotts of English goods. Sons of Liberty groups are hassling officials and disrupting business. Parliament is furious.

CRAM THE TAXES DOWN THEIR THROATS!

In the Virginia legislature, a young lawyer and dazzling orator named Patrick Henry attacks the king.

PATRICK HENRY

In those days, in Europe, the king was the father, the protector, the absolute and exalted ruler. You didn't mess with him.

33

"TREASON! TREASON!" CRY HORRIFIED LEGISLATORS.
PATRICK HENRY RESPONDS WITH:

IF THIS BE TREASON,
MAKE THE MOST OF IT!

GASP!

HENRY, TOO, DISCOVERS
THAT HIS LAW BUSINESS
INCREASES WITH HIS
NOTORIETY.

WITH THE COLONIES IN AN UPROAR, STAMPS
PREVENTED FROM BEING DISTRIBUTED, AND SHIPS
STUCK IN PORT, BUSINESS IS HURTING IN ENGLAND.

#6?!#

ALL SHIPS FROM
AMERICA
DELAYED!

IN 1766 PARLIAMENT CAVES IN AND REPEALS THE STAMP
TAX. IT SAVES FACE BY SAYING:

BUT WE HAVE
THE RIGHT TO
TAX YOU ANYTIME
WE LIKE!

THAT'S BULL!
WE WON.

34

LIFE IN THE COLONIES SEEMS TO CALM DOWN, BUT THE STAMP ACT CRISIS HAS CREATED A CORE GROUP OF RADICAL LEADERS-IN-TRAINING.

POLITICAL INDOCTRINATION

DISCIPLINING THE POPULAR WILL

HOW ABOUT DISCIPLINING THIS BROOM?

AND THE PEOPLE, WITH LITTLE FORMAL EDUCATION, START EDUCATING THEMSELVES ON THE ROLE OF GOVERNMENT.

ORDINARY PEOPLE CAN BE ELECTED BY ORDINARY PEOPLE WITH NO RESTRICTIONS ON VOTING.

SAM ADAMS ENLISTS TWO MORE MEN TO THE CAUSE. ONE IS JOHN HANCOCK, THE RICHEST YOUNG MAN IN BOSTON. (JOHN INHERITED HIS SHIPPING BUSINESS FROM HIS SMUGGLER UNCLE.)

JOHN, JOIN US AND YOU'LL BE GOVERNOR ONE DAY.

AND SAM RECRUITS HIS COUSIN, JOHN ADAMS.

JOHN IS A SHARP, AMBITIOUS HARVARD LAWYER WITH A BRAINY WIFE, ABIGAIL, AND A YOUNG FAMILY.

SAM, I'M NOT THE TYPE TO JOIN A MOB.

JOHN, THINK OF IT AS A CAREER MOVE.

JOHN ADAMS

IN 1767, THE NEW CHANCELLOR OF THE EXCHEQUER, "CHAMPAGNE CHARLIE TOWNSHEND" IS STILL SEARCHING FOR COLONIAL RICHES. HE TAXES IMPORTS AGAIN.

THE TOWNSHEND DUTIES

WE'RE HERE TO COLLECT THE KING'S TAXES.

OPERATING OUT OF BOSTON, THE CUSTOMS AGENTS GO RIGHT TO WORK STEALING FROM SAILORS AND HOLDING UP SHIPPERS.

YOU CUT US IN OR WE TURN YOU OVER TO THE COURTS.

THESE GUYS ARE BIGGER CROOKS THAN I EVER WAS.

AND TOWNSHEND IS INSISTING THAT THE COLONIES PAY TO SUPPORT BRITISH TROOPS ON THEIR SHORE.

WE DON'T WANT YOU HERE! WE CAN FIGHT INDIANS BETTER THAN YOU!

THESE NEW ACTIONS REAWAKEN THE ALLIANCE OF SAILORS, ARTISANS, LABORERS, AND MERCHANTS.

WE ARE FREE MEN

SAM, YOU NOTICE HOW BIG OUR CROWDS ARE GETTING, LATELY?

THIS IS THE OPPORTUNITY THE SONS OF LIBERTY HAVE BEEN WAITING FOR.

I'LL DO THE "TODAY A TAX ON SILK, TOMORROW SLAVERY" SPEECH.

I'LL DO "IF YOU'RE NOT WITH US, YOU'RE FOR TYRANNY."

RESIST

37

INSTANTLY, THE CUSTOMS OFFICIALS SCREAM FOR HELP FROM THE BRITISH MILITARY.

HOW DO WE KNOW IF IT'S A MOB?

IF THEY'RE AGAINST US, THEY'RE A MOB!

RESIST RACKETEERS

BY NOW, THE ARISTOCRATIC SOUTHERN PLANTERS BELIEVE THEIR PROFITS ARE THREATENED BY THE BRITISH.

WE COULD LOSE OUR RIGHTS, TOO.

THE SONS OF LIBERTY ARE GATHERING SUPPORT BUT THEY KNOW THEY HAVE TO BROADEN THEIR APPEAL.

MOB ACTION SCARES PEOPLE. AND WE NEED...

... ALL THE UNCOMMITTEDS, THE FARMERS, THE FRONTIER, AND THE SOUTH.

KEEP OUT DO NOT DISTURB NO ONE HOME

THEY CALL FOR AN ORGANIZED BOYCOTT OF ENGLISH GOODS.

SHOP AMERICAN

WEAR HOMESPUN NOT SILK

CURE STRESS WITH PEPPERMINT AND CHALK

LED BY SAM ADAMS, THE MASSACHUSETTS ASSEMBLY CALLS FOR SUPPORT FROM OTHER COLONIES AGAINST THE TOWNSHEND DUTIES. THE KING IS HORRIFIED.

THE RADICALS START FORMING THEIR OWN SHADOW ASSEMBLIES.

IN 1768, IN BOSTON, CUSTOMS AGENTS SEIZE A SHIP OWNED BY JOHN HANCOCK. A MOB ATTACKS THE AGENTS.

HANCOCK HIRES JOHN ADAMS TO DEFEND HIM AGAINST CHARGES OF SMUGGLING!

THE GOVERNOR OF MASSACHUSETTS TRIES TO BUY JOHN ADAMS WITH A BIG BUCKS JOB.

JOHN, YOU COULD BE THE KING'S ADVOCATE IN ADMIRALTY COURT. THINK OF YOUR FAMILY.

BUT JOHN HAS MADE HIS CHOICE. HE'S GAMBLING ON THE INSURGENTS.

HOW DO YOU LIKE IT, ABIGAIL?

I LIKE IT.

JOHN ADAMS — LAWYER TO THE RABBLE

ABIGAIL ADAMS AND JAMES OTIS' SISTER, MERCY, ARE POLITICALLY ASTUTE. BUT MEN BELIEVE THAT WOMEN'S PLACE IS IN THE HOME

JOHN, REMEMBER THE...

WE'RE BUSY, ABIGAIL!

JOHN ADAMS — LAWYER TO THE RABBLE

IN 1768, THE HARD-LINERS ARE IN CONTROL IN PARLIAMENT. TOWNSHEND IS DEAD AND LORD NORTH IS IN CHARGE. NORTH ORDERS BRITISH TROOPS INTO BOSTON.

WE'LL GET RID OF THE SONS OF LIBERTY AND THEIR ILLEGAL ASSEMBLIES ONCE AND FOR ALL!

THE BRITISH PRESENCE IN BOSTON IS GIVING THE CITY'S CIVILIANS STRESS ATTACKS.

SIMPLE MINDED TOOL OF THE RADICALS!

TURNCOAT BETRAYER OF YOUR COUNTRY!

TORY

PATRIOT

TARRED AND FEATHERED MERCHANT WHO IGNORED THE BOYCOTT.

MATTERS ARE MADE WORSE BY BRITISH SOLDIERS UNDERBIDDING LOCAL WORKERS FOR JOBS.

41

EVERYONE IS ON EDGE AND VULNERABLE TO TROUBLE BEING STIRRED UP BY SAM AND THE "SONS."

GO ON, THROW IT!

THE BOSTON MASSACRE

ONE SNOWY DAY IN 1770, A BRITISH SENTRY SMACKS A KID WHO'S BEEN TAUNTING HIM. THAT NIGHT A CLUB-SWINGING CROWD CONFRONTS THE SENTRIES.

CORNERED, THE SOLDIERS FIRE. FIVE CIVILIANS ARE KILLED. THEY INCLUDE AN IRISH IMMIGRANT, THE TEENAGE SON OF A GERMAN IMMIGRANT, AND AN AFRICAN NAMED CRISPUS ATTUCKS.

THE KILLINGS LAUNCH A NIGHT OF CHAOS AS ROVING BANDS OF CIVILIANS THREATEN EVEN THE HAUGHTY NEW GOVERNOR, HUTCHINSON.

TO CALM THE PEOPLE, HUTCHINSON CALLS FOR A TRIAL OF THE SOLDIERS.

LET THE RULE OF LAW DECIDE!

JOHN ADAMS AGREES TO DEFEND THE SOLDIERS.

HE'S THE PEOPLE'S LAWYER, WHAT'S HE DOING...

...DEFENDING THE ENEMY?

THE RADICAL LEADERS KNOW WHAT THEY'RE DOING.

JOHN WILL MAKE SURE NO ONE UNCOVERS WHO REALLY INSTIGATED THE TROUBLE.

43

THE WITNESSES TESTIFY AS EXPECTED.

THE SOLDIERS' LIVES WERE THREATENED. WHAT COULD THEY DO?

PEOPLE WERE JUST WALKING BY. THE SOLDIERS CAME AT THEM SCREAMING, "KILL, KILL!"

JOHN ADAMS SAYS:

THIS WAS A MOB OF KIDS, WISE GUYS, NEGROES, IRISH, SAILORS... THEY WERE NOT <u>REAL</u> BOSTONIANS...

...THE SOLDIERS WERE SIMPLY DEFENDING THEIR NATURAL RIGHT TO LIFE.

UP UNTIL NOW, THE CLERGY HAVE BEEN THE LEADERS IN COLONIAL LIFE AND THOUGHT. **O**N THIS DAY, JOHN MOVES LAWYERS TO THE FRONT OF THE STRUGGLE.

ONLY THROUGH THE LAW AND LAWYERS CAN TRUTH BE DISCOVERED AND EVIL PUNISHED.

THE RADICALS DRAGGED IN JOHN LOCKE WHENEVER IT SUITED THEM.

44

John gets the soldiers off. The radicals, understanding the value of a good sound bite, use the shooting as a rallying cry.

REMEMBER THE BOSTON MASSACRE!

In 1770, Lord North, the new Prime Minister, repeals the Townshend duties.

More trouble than they're worth...

...but we'll keep the duty on tea. What's the harm?

The merchants go back to business as usual, but England continues to harass her colonies and bypass colonial assemblies. England refuses to understand that her colonies now believe they have a right to reject Parliament.

If we're going to be taken advantage of, it'll be by someone we elect.

PUSHED BY SAM ADAMS, MASSACHUSETTS CRIES FOR COLONIAL COMMITTEES TO CRITICIZE BRITISH POLICIES.

VIRGINIA CALLS FOR A UNITING OF ALL THE COMMITTEES, AND THE COLONIES ARE OFFICIALLY LINKED IN ANGER.

BOSTON TEA PARTY

IN 1773, ENGLAND BLUNDERS AGAIN. THEY GIVE THE GRAFT-RIDDEN EAST INDIA COMPANY THE TEA MONOPOLY IN THE COLONIES.

WHEN THREE SHIPS FULL OF TEA ARRIVE IN BOSTON, A HUGE CROWD CALLS FOR THEM TO LEAVE. GOVERNOR HUTCHINSON, BY NOW A SYMBOL OF TORY VILLAINY IN BOSTON, REFUSES.

SAM ADAMS HAS A HIGH CONCEPT IDEA.

THAT NIGHT A GANG OF 150, IN WAR PAINT AND INDIAN DISGUISE, HEAD FOR THE HARBOR. RICH MERCHANT OR WHARF RAT, NO ONE IS IDENTIFIABLE.

I HEAR THAT THE INDIAN WITH THE RUFFLES IS JOHN HANCOCK HIMSELF.

BY MOONLIGHT, CHEERED BY A CROWD ON THE SHORE, THE BOGUS INDIANS TOSS THE TEA OVERBOARD.

JOHN ADAMS, WHO MANAGED TO BE OUT OF TOWN THAT NIGHT, LATER SAID:

IT WAS SUBLIME! MAJESTIC!

PARLIAMENT HAS LOST PATIENCE WITH THE COLONIAL BRATS. IT CLOSES THE PORT OF BOSTON AND SENDS IN GENERAL GAGE TO ESTABLISH MARTIAL LAW.

CLOSED

IN 1774, BRITAIN LOWERS THE BOUNDARIES OF HER PROVINCE OF QUEBEC TO THE OHIO RIVER. THE COLONIES FEEL THE NOOSE TIGHTENING.

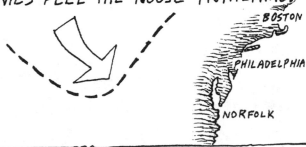

BOSTON

PHILADELPHIA

NORFOLK

FIRST CONTINENTAL CONGRESS

THE RADICAL LEADERS, BOSTON BRANCH, CALL FOR A MEETING OF ALL THE COLONIES. THEY SAY IT'S TO DISCUSS TRADE BOYCOTTS AGAINST BRITAIN, BUT CONSERVATIVE BUSINESSMEN ARE NERVOUS.

SAM ADAMS AND THE OTHER LUNATICS ARE GOING TO PUSH US INTO WAR.

WE'D BETTER SEND OUR PEOPLE TO THE MEETING TO HEAD OFF TROUBLE.

COLONISTS EVERYWHERE ARE FURIOUS OVER THE IMPOSITION OF MARTIAL LAW. THEY SEND AID TO BOSTON AND MEET TO DISCUSS THE WORSENING SITUATION.

THE COMMON PEOPLE SHOULD NOT BE ALLOWED TO DISCUSS THESE MATTERS.

BOSTON DOESN'T DESERVE THIS!

THE WORKING PEOPLE KNOW THAT ON ONE SIDE ARE THOSE WHO FEAR THE TROUBLE. ON THE OTHER SIDE ARE THOSE WHO WILL PROFIT FROM IT.

I'D RATHER BE ENSLAVED BY A RICH MAN THAN LED BY THE RIFFRAFF.

ONE THING IS CLEAR. IF THE DISTURBANCE LEADS TO WAR, IT'S THE PEOPLE IN THE MIDDLE WHO WILL DO MOST OF THE FIGHTING, AND MOST OF THE DYING.

IN 1774, 56 EDUCATED, CLEVER, WEALTHY, INFLUENTIAL LEADERS OF THE POSSIBLE NEW WORLD ORDER MEET IN PHILADELPHIA. THEY CHECK EACH OTHER OUT.

THE RADICALS DENY THEY'RE INTERESTED IN EXTREME ACTION. BUT THEY:

⭐ INFLAME PASSIONS BY DESCRIBING BRITISH ATROCITIES

BLOOD ALL OVER THE STREETS OF BOSTON.

⭐ ARM TWIST DELEGATES WITH DIRE THREATS

YOU KNOW WHAT IT FEELS LIKE TO BE RIDDEN OUT OF TOWN ON A RAIL?

⭐ OFFER DEALS TO PEOPLE WILLING TO UNITE WITH THEM

HOW'D YOU LIKE TO BE A GENERAL, GEORGE?

ONE WAY OR THE OTHER, THE MODERATES END UP VOTING WITH THE RADICALS.

WHEREAS, YOUR LOYAL SERVANTS ARE ENTITLED TO THE RIGHT OF CONSENT TO BE GOVERNED!

THIS CONGRESS HAS TAKEN POWER INTO ITS OWN HANDS. IT CALLS FOR A BOYCOTT, AND PUNISHMENT FOR ANYONE SUSPECTED OF VIOLATING THE BOYCOTT.

WHEN WE GET RID OF ENGLAND, EVERYONE WILL LIVE IN HARMONY.

MAYBE WE WON'T NEED COURTS.

GASP! SIR, YOU GO TOO FAR!

THE DELEGATES AGREE TO MEET THE NEXT YEAR. THE RADICALS ARE HAPPY. THE CONSERVATIVES ARE NOT.

JOHN, WE MAKE A GOOD TEAM.

PATRICK, YOU'RE RIGHT.

WE WERE TRICKED BY A BUNCH OF DEVIOUS SNAKES.

IN EVERY COLONY, COMMITTEES START CONVERTING GOOD-TIME MILITIAS INTO TRAINED MILITARY UNITS.

ATTEN-HUT!

ENGLAND VINDICTIVELY SABOTAGES NEW ENGLAND'S IMPORTANT FISHING INDUSTRY.

GENERAL GAGE IS UNDER PRESSURE TO PUNISH THE BOSTON AGITATORS. HE ORDERS A RAID ON A STOCKPILE OF WEAPONS AT CONCORD, 16 MILES FROM BOSTON.

LEXINGTON & CONCORD

THE BRITISH PREPARATIONS ARE QUICKLY SPOTTED BY THE PATRIOTS, WHO MAKE PLANS OF THEIR OWN.

ON THE NIGHT OF APRIL 18, 1775, 700 BRITISH SOLDIERS IN THEIR BOLD RED COATS SNEAK ACROSS THE CHARLES RIVER. EVERYONE BUT THE TROOPS KNOWS WHAT'S UP.

THEY'RE HEADING FOR CONCORD.

WITH A LIGHT IN THE OLD NORTH CHURCH, THE PATRIOTS SIGNAL ACROSS THE RIVER.

THE SECRET SIGNAL SAYS THE BRITISH ARE COMING BY WATER.

I CAN SEE THEY'RE COMING BY WATER!

HERE'S WHERE PAUL REVERE COMES INTO THE STORY. PAUL'S A SILVERSMITH TO THE RICH. HE'S ON HIS SECOND MARRIAGE, HE MAKES FALSE TEETH FOR TEENAGE GIRLS, AND HE'S A COURIER FOR THE RADICALS.

PAUL REVERE

PAUL, WE HAVE A RUSH JOB FOR YOU, WE'LL PAY EXTRA.

SUCCESS IN LIFE IS EASIER WITH TEETH BY REVERE

YOU GOT IT!

REVERE RIDES TO WARN SAM ADAMS AND JOHN HANCOCK. THEY ARE STAYING AT THE TOWN OF LEXINGTON ON THEIR WAY TO THE 2ND CONTINENTAL CONGRESS.

PAUL, AS YOU RIDE, YELL, "THE BRITISH ARE COMING, THE BRITISH ARE COMING!"

OKAY, OKAY!

AS THE ALARM SPREADS, PEOPLE HIDE THEIR VALUABLES AND REACH FOR THEIR GUNS.

AT LEXINGTON, REVERE COMPLETES HIS JOB. THE MILITIA, CALLED MINUTE MEN, FALL IN. SAM AND JOHN FALL OUT.

WE'RE LEADERS NOT FIGHTERS.

AS DAWN BREAKS, THE 700 BRITISH TROOPS TOP A HILL OVERLOOKING LEXINGTON GREEN. ON THE GREEN STAND 75 NERVOUS MILITIA.

WHY ARE WE CALLED MINUTE MEN?

BECAUSE IN A MINUTE I'M OUTTA HERE.

THE BRITISH MAJOR OF MARINES STARTS DOWN THE HILL SCREAMING:

DISPERSE, YE VILLAINS, DISPERSE!

DISPERSE IS JUST WHAT THE MINUTE MEN TRY TO DO. BUT SOMEONE FIRES A SHOT. SUDDENLY, THE WHOLE BRITISH FORCE IS OUT OF CONTROL, RACING DOWN THE HILL, <u>GUNS BLASTING.</u>

WHEN THE SMOKE CLEARS, THERE ARE EIGHT DEAD MINUTE MEN ON LEXINGTON GREEN. THE BRITISH ARE BACK UNDER CONTROL AND ARE PROUDLY MARCHING TOWARD CONCORD.

AT NORTH BRIDGE, NERVOUS REDCOATS FIRE ON THE THREATENING FARMERS. UNLIKE AT LEXINGTON, THE FARMERS FIRE BACK. MEN FALL ON BOTH SIDES.

THE SURROUNDING HILLS ARE FILLING WITH ANGRY FARMERS. THE BRITISH CALL FOR A RETREAT BACK TO BOSTON.

THE COLONISTS FOLLOW, FIRING FROM BEHIND ROCKS, TREES, AND FENCES,

THE REBELLION AGAINST ENGLAND HAS NOW SPREAD TO THE COUNTRYSIDE.

BOOM!

BLAST!

BAM!

LIKE SHADOWS, THE FARMERS FIRE, RELOAD, MOVE, AND FIRE. THE ENGLISH ARE DRIVEN MAD BY THE RELENTLESS CROSSFIRE.

BATTERED AND BEATEN, THE BRITISH FINALLY REACH THE SAFETY OF BOSTON HARBOR. AND A LEADERLESS COUNTRY MOB HAS WON A CLEAR VICTORY OVER THE KING'S FINEST.

THE PATRIOT LEADERS, NERVOUS YET JUBILANT, SPREAD THE WORD. THE ROADS AROUND BOSTON...

...QUICKLY FILL WITH VOLUNTEERS CARRYING KETTLES, PITCHFORKS, AND MUSKETS. THEY'RE WEARING HOMEMADE UNIFORMS AND HAVE COME TO FIGHT FOR LIBERTY AND THEIR POCKETBOOKS.

AS THIS MOTLEY CREW SURROUNDS BOSTON, IN ENGLAND, KING GEORGE III THREATENS:

THEY WILL REGRET THIS DAY!

2

1775 - 1781

REDCOATS & GUERRILLAS

2ND CONTINENTAL CONGRESS

IN MAY, 1775, CONGRESS MEETS AGAIN IN PHILADELPHIA. THE REBELLION IS OFFICIAL AND EVERYONE FEELS HEROIC.

IF WE'RE NOW A COUNTRY, THE VOLUNTEERS AROUND BOSTON ARE OUR ARMY.

THEREFORE, WE NEED GENERALS!

CONGRESS CHOOSES A DELEGATE FROM VIRGINIA, GEORGE WASHINGTON, AS ITS COMMANDER-IN-CHIEF.

POSSIBLE REASONS WHY GEORGE IS CHOSEN.

☆ HE'S THE ONLY DELEGATE WEARING A UNIFORM. (HE FOUGHT IN THE FRENCH AND INDIAN WAR.)

☆ HE'S A RICH PLANTATION OWNER. (HE MARRIED A WEALTHY WOMAN.)

☆ IT'S POLITICALLY IMPORTANT TO APPOINT A SOUTHERNER.

☆ HE ALREADY LOOKS LIKE A STATUE.

GEORGE WASHINGTON SETS OUT FOR BOSTON TO TAKE COMMAND. MEANWHILE, AT BOSTON, THE REBEL LEADERS DECIDE TO FORTIFY **BUNKER HILL** WHICH GUARDS THE CHARLES RIVER.

AT NIGHT THE CHIEFTAINS LEAD THEIR VOLUNTEERS UP THE WRONG HILL.

ARE YOU SURE THIS IS THE RIGHT PATH?

OF COURSE!

ALL NIGHT THEY BUILD DEFENSES.

CHOP, CHOP

BAM, BAM

CRASH, OUCH!

AT DAWN THEY DISCOVER THEY'RE ON BREED'S HILL AND EXPOSED TO THE WHOLE BRITISH ARMY AND NAVY. THE BRITISH GENERAL, HOWE, LOVES IT!

HA! LOOK AT WHAT THOSE FARMERS HAVE DONE NOW!

UH, OH, THAT'S BUNKER HILL BEHIND US.

HOWE ORGANIZES HIS SOLDIERS IN TRADITIONAL LINES AND, TO THE BEAT OF DRUMS, MARCHES THEM UP BREED'S HILL. THE RESIDENTS OF BOSTON WATCH FROM THE ROOFTOPS.

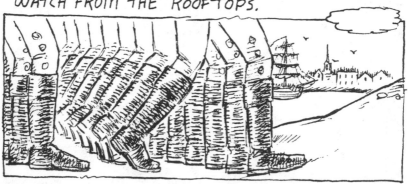

THE COLONIAL FORCES HAVE FEW PLANS, SUPPLIES, OR LEADERS. BUT THEY HAVE A BIT OF DIRT TO HIDE BEHIND AND HUNTERS' INSTINCTS.

SHOOT AT THEIR OFFICERS FIRST.

YEAH. PRETEND THEY'RE WILD TURKEYS.

HOLD YOUR FIRE TILL YOU CAN COUNT THEIR BUTTONS.

THIS WAS UNHEARD OF. NO EUROPEAN OFFICER WOULD EVER TELL HIS PEASANT SOLDIERS TO SHOOT AT ENEMY OFFICERS. ALL OFFICERS WERE ARISTOCRATS.

THE TRADITIONAL EUROPEAN SOLDIER IS ABOUT TO MEET DANIEL BOONE.

WHEN THE BRITISH ARE ALMOST ON TOP OF THEM, THE REBELS START **FIRING**

IT'S A BLOODY DISASTER FOR THE BRITISH. BUT HOWE KEEPS SENDING HIS TROOPS BACK TILL HALF OF THEM ARE DEAD. THE REBELS FINALLY RUN OUT OF AMMUNITION AND ARE REDUCED TO THROWING ROCKS AND SCREAMING FOR HELP.

HELP! BACKUP! SUPPORT! WHERE IS EVERYBODY?

SHOULDN'T WE HELP THEM?

I DON'T KNOW!

I THINK WE SHOULD STAY HERE.

WHAT'S LEFT OF HOWE'S TROOPS REACH THE COLONIAL LINES. THE MILITIA RUN. BUT THEY HAVE WON AN AWESOME PSYCHOLOGICAL VICTORY OVER THE GREATEST EUROPEAN MILITARY POWER OF THE DAY.

UNFORTUNATELY, THE REBELS HAVE THE FALSE IMPRESSION THAT THEY CAN HANDLE THE BRITISH ARMY.

WE WERE ON THE WRONG HILL, HAD LITTLE AMMUNITION, AND STILL BEAT THEM.

GEORGE WASHINGTON

WASHINGTON ARRIVES TO TAKE OVER THE ARMY. HE'S FROM THE SOUTHERN ELITE, USED TO BEING OBEYED BY THE LOWER CLASSES AND THE SERVANTS AND SLAVES.

DISCIPLINE AND OBEDIENCE WIN WARS!

HE FINDS NOT AN ARMY, BUT FARMERS, SHOPKEEPERS, ITINERANT WORKERS, WOMEN, AFRICANS, AND TEENAGERS LED BY OFFICERS WHO GOT COMMISSIONS THROUGH PULL.

WASHINGTON ESPECIALLY DISLIKES THE NEW ENGLANDERS.

NASTY, CRAFTY PEOPLE WITH UGLY ACCENTS.

WHINE, WHINE

NO ONE KNOWS HOW TO TAKE ORDERS.

39 LASHES FOR INSUBORDINATION!

LIGHTEN UP, GEORGE. I WENT FOR A LITTLE WALK.

CARRYING THE DEADLY, NEW, LONG RIFLES ARE SOUTHERN, BUCKSKIN-CLAD PRIMA DONNAS.

THEY'RE OUR RIFLES. WE'LL DECIDE WHEN TO FIRE THEM. AND WE DON'T DO KP.

THE VOLUNTEERS DON'T EVEN LIKE EACH OTHER.

I'LL FIGHT FOR LIBERTY! BUT NO WAY WILL I SALUTE A GUY FROM NEW JERSEY.

SIGH

MEANWHILE, THE REBEL LEADERS KNOW THAT, TO FIGHT A WAR, YOU NEED ARTILLERY. AND THE ONLY WAY TO GET CANNON QUICKLY IS TO STEAL THEM.

THE BRITISH HAVE LOTS OF CANNON AT FORT TICONDEROGA IN UPSTATE NEW YORK.

SOME OF THE COLONISTS ARE ANXIOUS TO START THE FIGHTING. TWO OF THESE ARE:

ETHAN ALLEN— LOUDMOUTHED LEADER OF THE GREEN MOUNTAIN BOYS OF VERMONT.

AND

BENEDICT ARNOLD — BUSINESSMAN- TURNED- RUTHLESS, AMBITIOUS SOLDIER.

I'M AUTHORIZED BY MASSACHUSETTS.

I'M AUTHORIZED BY CONNECTICUT.

BOTH LUST TO BE THE CONQUEROR OF TICONDEROGA

IN MAY, 1775, AT THE HEAD OF THE SAME TROOPS, ALLEN AND ARNOLD CHARGE THE DILAPIDATED FORT.

I'M FIRST!

I'M FIRST!

ZZZ

THEY EASILY CAPTURE THE FEW SLEEPY BRITS AND THE CANNON. THE REAL BATTLE IS BETWEEN ALLEN AND ARNOLD FIGHTING FOR COMMAND.

IN THE SPRING OF 1775, CONGRESS ORDERS A FORCE INTO CANADA TO CHALLENGE THE BRITISH AND ENCOURAGE CANADIANS TO JOIN THE REBELLION. BUT THE GENERALS WASTE THE GOOD WEATHER.

EVENTUALLY, BRAVE, HANDSOME GENERAL GEORGE MONTGOMERY TAKES COMMAND AND LEADS HIS MEN INTO THE NORTHERN WINTER.

WASHINGTON SENDS BENEDICT ARNOLD ON A HELLISH 500 MILE MARCH THROUGH MAINE TO MEET UP WITH MONTGOMERY. ARNOLD'S MEN ARE FORCED TO DRAG THEIR SUPPLIES OVER TREACHEROUS TERRAIN. SOME OF THE MEN DIE IN THE ICY STREAMS AND SWAMPS. THE OTHERS PERSEVERE.

THE RELENTLESS ARNOLD AND HALF HIS ORIGINAL FORCE MEET UP WITH MONTGOMERY AT THE SAINT LAWRENCE RIVER. THEY PLAN A TWO-PRONGED ATTACK UP THE TOWERING CLIFFS OF QUEBEC CITY.

ON A JANUARY NIGHT, IN A BLIZZARD, A BRITISH SENTRY SEES SHADOWS THROUGH THE BLINDING SNOW. HE **FIRES**.

THE FIRST BURST KILLS THE DASHING MONTGOMERY. HIS SHOCKED MEN RETREAT AND THIS ACTION IS OVER BEFORE IT BEGINS.

ARNOLD AND HIS TROOPS RUN INTO A BRITISH TRAP. A MUSKET BALL BREAKS ARNOLD'S LEG. HE ENDS UP IN A HOSPITAL BED A MILE AWAY, SCREAMING ORDERS, AS HIS HARD-FIGHTING MEN ARE ROUTED BY BRITISH FIRE.

WHAT'S LEFT OF THE CONTINENTAL SOLDIERS LEAVE CANADA BEHIND AND STAGGER SOUTH. AND THE CANADIANS NEVER DO JOIN THE WAR FOR INDEPENDENCE.

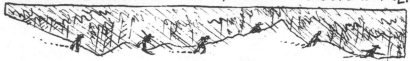

THE REAL HERO OF THE WINTER IS BIG, FAT FORMER BOOKSELLER HENRY KNOX. KNOX DRAGS ALL THE TICONDEROGA CANNON BACK THROUGH THE THICK FORESTS TO WASHINGTON'S CAMP OUTSIDE BOSTON.

HANK, FROM NOW ON YOU'RE MY HEAD OF ARTILLERY.

IN MARCH, 1776, WASHINGTON LINES UP THE CANNON ON DORCHESTER HEIGHTS OVER-LOOKING BOSTON. THE BRITISH GENERAL, HOWE, DECIDES TO LEAVE.

THEY'RE ALL CRAZY HERE. IT WOULD BE SMARTER TO FINISH THEM OFF IN NEW YORK WHERE THERE ARE LOTS OF TORIES!

74

BY NOW THE COLONISTS ARE BEING TORN APART BY FEAR AND DISSENSION.

THE BRITISH ARE OFFERING FREEDOM AND REWARDS TO SLAVES AND INDIANS WHO REVOLT.

WE'LL BE SCALPED IN THE STREETS!

BUGLE
SLAVES INDIANS JOIN BRITISH

IN CONGRESS, THE RADICALS, WITH JOHN ADAMS NOW IN THE LEAD, BATTLE THE CONSERVATIVES.

WE MUST BE A FREE AND INDEPENDENT CONFEDERATION OF STATES!

WE NEED TO BE REUNITED WITH ENGLAND BEFORE THE LOWER CLASSES OVER-RUN US!

THE AVERAGE CITIZEN CAN'T EVEN AGREE ON WHAT THE TROUBLE IS ABOUT.

POWER PROFIT

PATRIOTISM

THE RADICAL LEADERS ARE FRUSTRATED.

WHAT'S IT GOING TO TAKE TO GET THE WHOLE COUNTRY BEHIND THE IDEA OF INDEPENDENCE?

IN THE 1700s, MANY PEOPLE STILL BELIEVE IN THE HEREDITARY RIGHT OF KINGS TO RULE.

OUR PROBLEM IS WITH A GREEDY PARLIAMENT AND ITS AGENTS...

...BUT SEPARATE FROM THE KING? OH, GOD, NO!

FERRY LANDING

THEN, THE RADICALS GET A BREAK. IN 1774, A 37-YEAR-OLD ENGLISH IMMIGRANT SHOWED UP IN PHILADELPHIA. HE LEFT BEHIND FAILED JOBS, AND FAILED MARRIAGES, AND CAME LOOKING FOR A NEW LIFE. HIS NAME IS

TOM PAINE

TOM PAINE KNOWS FIRSTHAND THE TYRANNY OF THE ENGLISH ELITE AND THE GRINDING POVERTY OF THE LOWER CLASSES.

AND HE KNOWS HOW TO WRITE!

TOM LANDS A JOB ON A PHILADELPHIA MAGAZINE. HE WRITES ESSAYS ATTACKING SLAVERY AND THE REPRESSION OF WOMEN. THE RADICALS IN CONGRESS NOTICE HIS WORK AND HAVE A TALK WITH HIM.

PAINE, FORGET SLAVES AND WOMEN. WRITE ABOUT INDEPENDENCE — THAT'S WHERE THE ACTION IS.

ADVERTISING →
← EDITORIAL

TOM PAINE LISTENS AND, WITH A BOTTLE OF RUM AT HIS ELBOW, HE GOES TO WORK.

PAINE, EASY ON THE RUM AND THE "DEMOCRACY" STUFF.

ROOMS

TO A LOT OF COLONISTS, "DEMOCRACY" IS ANOTHER WORD FOR "MOB."

EARLY IN 1776, TOM COMES OUT WITH A PAMPHLET HE CALLS

IT'S WRITTEN SIMPLY AND DIRECTLY WITHOUT THE FLOURISHES THE POWERFUL USE TO OBSCURE THE TRUTH.

COMMON SENSE
TO INHABITANTS OF AMERICA
* ORIGIN OF GOVERNMENT
* MONARCHY
* STATE OF AFFAIRS
* REFLECT

COMMON SENSE ATTACKS THE WHOLE BRITISH SYSTEM, INCLUDING THE KING AND HEREDITARY PRIVILEGE.

THE PAMPHLET HITS PEOPLE IN THE GUT. IT'S A RUNAWAY BEST-SELLER FROM CITY TO FRONTIER.

TOM'S WORDS OPEN THE EYES OF THE RICH, THE POOR, THE YOUNG, THE OLD. THE TIMING IS PERFECT! RADICALISM BECOMES FASHIONABLE.

JOHN ADAMS AND SOME OF THE OTHER FUTURE FOUNDING FATHERS CRITICIZE TOM AND HIS WORDS.

PAINE DIDN'T PUT HIS NAME ON THE BOOK, HE ISN'T GETTING ANY ROYALTIES, AND HE'S ENLISTING IN THE ARMY AS A PRIVATE. IS THAT COMMON SENSE?

HE SAYS PEOPLE ARE BASICALLY GOOD. BUT THEY'RE NOT. THEY'RE BASICALLY **GREEDY**. HE'S NAIVE!

AND HE HAS NO FAMILY CONNECTIONS.

BUT, HEY, HE'S GOTTEN PEOPLE BEHIND THE IDEA OF INDEPENDENCE.

RIGHT! FIRST WE WIN A SHORT, VIOLENT WAR. THEN WE WORRY ABOUT TOO MUCH DEMOCRACY.

BEFORE THIS, REVOLUTION MEANT PLANETS TURNING IN SPACE. NOW IT'LL ALSO MEAN OVERTHROWING A GOVERNMENT.

THE DECLARATION OF ★ INDEPENDENCE ★

IN JUNE, 1776, RICHARD HENRY LEE, DELEGATE FROM VIRGINIA, BLUE BLOOD, AND RADICAL, STANDS UP IN CONGRESS AND PROPOSES A RESOLUTION...

...THAT THESE COLONIES ARE *FREE* AND *INDEPENDENT STATES!*

IN A SWELTERING PHILADELPHIA, THE DELEGATES SWEAT, SWAT FLIES, AND ARGUE INDEPENDENCE.

BUSINESSES WILL BE DESTROYED. THE PEOPLE CAN'T BE TRUSTED.

WAP!

BUT WE'LL HAVE A WRITTEN CONSTITUTION AND LAWS TO PROTECT EVERYONE.

I VOTE WE ADJOURN FOR A COOL DRINK.

I SECOND THAT.

SINCE WE'RE VOTING FOR INDEPENDENCE, WE SHOULD COMPOSE A DECLARATION OF OUR REASONS FOR ARMING.

OH, IT'S NOT THAT IMPORTANT. GIVE THE JOB TO JEFFERSON.

DRAGON TAVERN

THOMAS JEFFERSON, VIRGINIA GENTLEMAN, SCIENTIST, MUSICIAN, GOURMET, ARCHITECT, VISIONARY, STYLISH WRITER, AND IDEALIST. HE'S FAR AHEAD OF THE COUNTRY IN PUSHING FOR EQUALITY FOR ALL PEOPLE, INCLUDING SLAVES (YET HE NEVER FREES HIS OWN SLAVES).

THOMAS JEFFERSON

TOM, WRITE US SOMETHING DIGNIFIED YET MAGICAL.

BORROWING FROM THE ENLIGHTENMENT AND THE NEW VIRGINIA BILL OF RIGHTS, TOM WRITES AN ELOQUENT STATEMENT OF BELIEFS.

INALIENABLE OR UNALIENABLE, HMMM...?

When in the course of human events it becomes necessary

OF COURSE, ADAMS, FRANKLIN, AND THE OTHER DELEGATES HAVE TO EDIT HIM.

ON JULY 2, 1776, WITH NEWS OF THE ARRIVAL OF BRITISH WARSHIPS IN NEW YORK, AND UNDER PRESSURE FROM THE RADICALS, THE DELEGATES VOTE FOR INDEPENDENCE. ON JULY 4, THEY ADOPT THE **D**ECLARATION OF **I**NDEPENDENCE.

AND SO, USING FAITH IN A COMMON HUMANITY AS A CALL TO ACTION, THE COLONIES REVOLT AGAINST THEIR OWN GOVERNMENT...

... WE MUTUALLY PLEDGE TO EACH OTHER OUR LIVES...

WE ARE DOOMED!

WE ARE FREE!

... AND ANNOUNCE THAT THEY ARE OFFICIALLY AVAILABLE FOR FUNDS AND WEAPONS FROM ANY COUNTRY THAT WANTS TO HELP DEFEAT ENGLAND.

THE COLONIES, NOW CALLED STATES, GO TO WORK ON STATE AND NATIONAL CONSTITUTIONS, AND THEY QUICKLY ORGANIZE MILITARY DRAFTS. THE PEOPLE WATCH SUSPICIOUSLY TO SEE HOW MANY RIGHTS AND FREEDOMS THEY'LL BE GUARANTEED UNDER THE NEW ORDER.

LONG ISLAND TO TRENTON

IN THE SPRING OF 1776, CONGRESS HAD SENT GEORGE WASHINGTON AND HIS RAGGEDY CONTINENTAL ARMY SOUTH TO PREPARE A DEFENSE OF NEW YORK CITY.

Now, IN NEW YORK, THE PATRIOTS EYE THE FLOTILLA OF WARSHIPS FULL OF TRAINED BRITISH TROOPS AND GERMAN MERCENARIES SENT BY KING GEORGE III TO PUT A QUICK END TO THIS WAR.

WASHINGTON BLUNDERS. HE SPLITS HIS ARMY BETWEEN MANHATTAN AND LONG ISLAND. GENERAL HOWE AIMS FOR LONG ISLAND. HE DEPLOYS HIS TROOPS, FLANKS THE REBELS, AND CRUSHES THEM. THOSE WHO ESCAPE ARE TRAPPED ON BROOKLYN HEIGHTS.

ALL LOOKS LOST TILL WASHINGTON DISCOVERS A SECRET WEAPON: AMONG HIS TROOPS ARE TOUGH FISHERMEN FROM MARBLEHEAD, MASSACHUSETTS. (SOME OF THE FISHERMEN ARE AFRICANS, THOUGH, OFFICIALLY, AFRICANS ARE BANNED FROM THE MILITARY.)

ALL NIGHT, IN RAIN AND FOG, AND UNDER THE NOSES AND GUNS OF THE BRITISH AND GERMANS, THE FISHERMEN SECRETLY FERRY THE REBELS BACK ACROSS THE EAST RIVER TO MANHATTAN ISLAND.

BY MORNING, THE CONTINENTALS HAVE ESCAPED.

INSTEAD OF CUTTING HIS LOSSES AND RETREATING, WASHINGTON DECIDES TO DEFEND MANHATTAN — NOT THAT TORY NEW YORK HAS ANY LIKING FOR THE REBELS.

ENGLISH WARSHIPS SAIL UP THE EAST RIVER AND LET LOOSE A THUNDEROUS CANNONADE DOWN ON THE CONTINENTALS DUG IN ON THE SHORE.

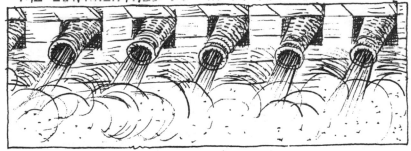

IN THE MIDDLE OF THE BOMBARDMENT, HOWE RELEASES HIS SCREAMING, STABBING, SHOOTING TROOPS.

THIS ONSLAUGHT SCARES THE HELL OUT OF THE REBEL ARMY. THEY DROP EVERYTHING AND RUN TOWARD HARLEM HEIGHTS FOLLOWED BY A FURIOUS WASHINGTON.

COWARDS! INCOMPETENTS!

GEORGE SHOULD HAVE LIGHTENED UP. THESE WERE BRAVE CIVILIANS WHO HAD NEVER FACED AN AERIAL BARRAGE BEFORE.

WASHINGTON GETS THE POINT. TO STAY ALIVE HE MUST RETREAT. HE LEADS THE CONTINENTAL ARMY NORTH. THEY SURVIVE THE BATTLE OF WHITE PLAINS AND CROSS THE HUDSON RIVER INTO NEW JERSEY. THEY'RE FOLLOWED BY A SMUG GENERAL HOWE.

THIS IS WHERE HOWE OVERWHELMS THE REBEL DEFENDERS AND DESTROYS FORT WASHINGTON AND FORT LEE GUARDING THE HUDSON.

WASHINGTON HATES THE INDIVIDUALISM THAT COMES NATURALLY TO HIS MEN. BUT THERE'S ONE REBEL GENERAL, CHARLES LEE, A FORMER BRITISH OFFICER, WHO SUPPORTS THE IDEA OF A CIVILIAN ARMY.

A GUERRILLA ARMY IS A DISOBEDIENT ARMY.

THAT'S NOT DISOBEDIENCE, IT'S STRENGTH AND INDEPENDENCE, YOU BOOB.

LEE, AN ODD CHARACTER, ALSO THINKS WASHINGTON IS INEPT AND TRIES TO UNDERMINE HIS AUTHORITY. BUT HIS EFFORTS END WHEN HE'S CAPTURED BY A BRITISH PLATOON WHILE HE'S PARTYING WITH A BARMAID.

White's Tavern

IT'S WINTER IN NEW JERSEY AND THE CONTINENTAL ARMY IS IN TROUBLE. THE SUPPLIES ARE FEW, AND THE SOLDIERS ARE SICK, STARVING, AND DESERTING.

WHERE'S MY ARMY?

SIR, I SENT THE ONES STILL HERE AFTER THE ONES WHO'VE LEFT.

THE ARMY IS IN TATTERS AND LEAVING BLOODY FOOTPRINTS IN THE SNOW. THE PEOPLE WHO ONCE BELIEVED IN THE REBELLION ARE THINKING IT'S FOOLHARDY. LOCAL PATRIOTS ARE DISAPPEARING.

WHERE'S OUR REVOLUTIONARY COMMITTEE?

NO ONE'S HOME, SIR.

KNOCK KNOCK

SHHH

AT ANY GIVEN TIME, ONE THIRD OF THE POPULATION WAS FOR THE WAR, ONE THIRD WAS AGAINST IT, AND ONE THIRD TRIED TO STAY NEUTRAL.

TOM PAINE, AN ENLISTED MAN WITH WASHINGTON'S ARMY, WRITES:

THESE ARE THE TIMES THAT TRY MEN'S SOULS

WITH THE BRITISH GENERAL, CORNWALLIS, IN PURSUIT, WASHINGTON AND HIS DWINDLING ARMY CROSS THE DELAWARE RIVER INTO PENNSYLVANIA.

IN NEARBY PHILADELPHIA, CONGRESS WORRIES ABOUT ITS OWN NECK. IT GIVES WASHINGTON FULL POWER TO RUN THE WAR AND CATCHES THE FIRST HORSES OUT OF TOWN.

I ALWAYS KNEW WASHINGTON WAS A POOR CHOICE.

BUT IT'S THE MIDDLE OF WINTER AND CORNWALLIS IS COLD. HE LEAVES A FEW OUTPOSTS AND HEADS BACK TO THE WARMTH OF HIS MISTRESS IN NEW YORK.

THE REBELS WILL BE DEAD BY SPRING, ANYWAY.

WASHINGTON IS DESPERATE FOR A VICTORY. HE COMES UP WITH A DARING, COMPLICATED PLAN FOR AN ATTACK ON A TRENTON, NEW JERSEY, OUTPOST.

91

ON THE NIGHT OF DECEMBER 25, 1776, THE MARBLEHEAD FISHERMEN ROW HENRY KNOX'S CANNON AND WHAT'S LEFT OF THE CONTINENTAL ARMY BACK ACROSS THE ICE-CLOGGED DELAWARE RIVER.

THE HALF-FROZEN REBELS SURPRISE A CAMP OF SLEEPING GERMANS. WITH CANNON AND BAYONETS (THEY'RE USING BAYONETS FOR THE FIRST TIME) THEY DEMOLISH THE GERMANS.

WASHINGTON LEADS HIS EXHAUSTED MEN AWAY FROM THE BATTLEFIELD. IT'S A MINOR VICTORY BUT IT STRENGTHENS THE PEOPLE'S PATRIOTISM AND BRINGS CONGRESS OUT OF HIDING.

OURS IS A GREAT CAUSE.

I KNEW WASHINGTON WAS OUR MAN.

SARATOGA

EARLY IN 1777, KING GEORGE AND HIS CRONIES COME UP WITH A NEW PLAN TO END THE WAR.

WE'LL SEND AN ARMY FROM CANADA DOWN THE HUDSON RIVER. THEY'LL MEET WITH HOWE COMING UP FROM NEW YORK.

THAT'LL CRUSH THE BUMPKINS...

...BETWEEN THE HAMMER AND THE ANVIL.

THEY GIVE THE COMMAND TO GENERAL "GENTLEMAN JOHNNY" BURGOYNE.

JOHN, THE TORIES AND THE SAVAGES WILL SURELY JOIN UP WITH YOU.

NO PROBLEM.

GENTLEMAN JOHNNY PUTS TOGETHER A FULL-BLOWN EUROPEAN-STYLE ARMY WITH BANDS, CANNON, AN OFFICER CORPS FORMED FROM THE EUROPEAN ARISTOCRACY, HIS WINE CELLAR, AND HIS MISTRESS.

WE ARE THE MESSENGERS OF JUSTICE AND WRATH!

HE CALLS FOR TORIES AND INDIAN TRIBES TO JOIN HIM. THE TORIES DO NOT. SOME INDIAN TRIBES DO.

THE GREAT WHITE FATHER FROM ACROSS THE SEA INVITES YOU TO A GENTLEMANLY WAR WITH MUCH PLUNDER.

THIS MIGHT BE A WAY TO GET OUR LAND BACK.

AS THE U.S. GENERALS ARGUE OVER WHO WILL LEAD THEIR DEFENSE, BURGOYNE TAKES FORT TICONDEROGA AND HEADS SOUTH TOWARD ALBANY.

WE ARE THE HAMMER.

BUT IT'S HEAVY GOING FOR THE REDCOATS. THE FORESTS ARE THICK AND THE LOCAL MILITIA ARE STARTING TO FOLLOW AND HARASS THEM, GUERRILLA STYLE.

WHILE HIS INDIAN ALLIES DISAPPEAR, BURGOYNE AND HIS OFFICERS IGNORE THE DANGER SIGNS...

THE REBEL PRESSURE IS INCREASING AND BURGOYNE IS FORCED TO BURY HIS DEAD QUICKLY. HE LEAVES ARMS AND LEGS STICKING ABOVE THE GROUND...TO BECOME FOOD FOR WILD ANIMALS.

IN AUGUST THE BRITISH ARE SHOCKED WHEN A TROOP OF FORAGING GERMANS IS DEFEATED AT BENNINGTON, VERMONT, BY LOCAL REBEL FARMERS.

THEN, A MESSAGE ARRIVES FROM GENERAL HOWE.

AT FREEMAN'S FARM, NEAR SARATOGA, NEW YORK, SOUTHERN MARKSMEN HIDE IN TREES, COMMUNICATING BY GOBBLING LIKE WILD TURKEYS. WITH LONG RIFLES, THEY CATCH THE REDCOATS IN DEADLY FIRE.

BACK IN PENNSYLVANIA, WASHINGTON FAILS TO KEEP HOWE FROM PHILADELPHIA.

MEN! YOU DIDN'T FOLLOW MY PLANS.

CONGRESS LEAVES TOWN AGAIN.

MEANWHILE, IN PARIS, OLD BEN FRANKLIN, GRANDFATHER TO THE REVOLUTION, SEEKS MONEY AND SUPPORT FOR THE YOUNG COUNTRY. HE'S A HOMESPUN PHILOSOPHER, SCIENTIST, INVENTOR, PUBLISHER, SHREWD STATESMAN, CONSTANT PHILANDERER, AND THE ONLY INTERNATIONAL STAR AMONG THE FOUNDING FATHERS.

EARLY TO BED AND EARLY TO RISE MAKE A MAN HEALTHY, WEALTHY, AND WISE.

OH, BEN, YOU'RE SUCH A SAVAGE.

NEVER LEAVE TO TOMORROW WHAT YOU CAN DO TODAY.

BENJAMIN FRANKLIN

97

OUTSIDE SARATOGA, THE KING'S PLAN TO SPLIT THE COLONIES FINALLY DIES. IN THE U.S. COMMAND TENT, THE NEW GENERAL IN CHARGE, GATES, AND GENERAL BENEDICT ARNOLD FIGHT OVER STRATEGY.

ON THE FIELD, THE REBEL SOLDIERS HIT, RUN, AND IMPROVISE. THEY DESTROY THE MORE INFLEXIBLE BRITISH AS A FIGHTING FORCE.

A MAJOR INVADING ARMY HAS BEEN WIPED OUT BY A NATIVE FORCE THAT USES THE TERRAIN, TRAVELS LIGHT, AND EATS ROOTS.

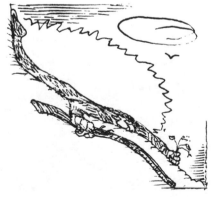

AFTER THE SURRENDER, WHAT'S LEFT OF THE BRITISH ARMY SEE THEIR OPPONENTS FOR THE FIRST TIME: MEN AND WOMEN, OLD AND YOUNG, BLACK AND WHITE, IMMIGRANTS AND OLD-LINE FAMILIES, ALL THE UNRULY COLONISTS FINALLY PULLING TOGETHER.

IN FRANCE, THEY MAKE PLANS TO HELP THE REBELS, THE ENEMY OF THEIR ENEMY. IN ENGLAND, THE KING'S SCREAMING THAT IT'S ALL BURGOYNE'S FAULT. IN SARATOGA, GATES IS TAKING CREDIT FOR THE VICTORY.

TAKE A LETTER TO CONGRESS, "HOW I DEFEATED GENERAL BURGOYNE..."

DON'T BOTHER SENDING A COPY TO WASHINGTON.

IN THE MILITARY AND IN CONGRESS, SOME ARE BUSILY ATTACKING THE COMMANDER-IN-CHIEF.

I'LL NEVER BE PROMOTED TILL WASHINGTON IS GONE.

HE'S AN INEPT FOOL WHO NEVER LISTENS.

HE WANTS TO BE KING!

WASHINGTON DISPLAYS A GREATER TALENT FOR POLITICAL COMBAT THAN FOR MILITARY TACTICS. HE DEFEATS THOSE TRYING TO DISCREDIT HIM.

WASHINGTON HAS ENEMIES AMONG THE POWERFUL BUT HE'S BEGINNING TO BE SEEN BY THE PEOPLE AS A SYMBOL OF THE STRENGTH OF THE COUNTRY.

GEORGE IS A ROCK!

IN NOVEMBER, 1777, CONGRESS ADOPTS THE ARTICLES OF CONFEDERATION. THE NEW COUNTRY NOW HAS A CENTRAL GOVERNMENT... OF SORTS. THE STATES REMAIN SUSPICIOUS OF CENTRALIZED AUTHORITY.

IT'S NOT FAIR! WE IN CONGRESS HAVE TO GO TO THE STATES FOR TAX MONEY AND TO RAISE AN ARMY.

BUT WE HAVE THE POWER TO PRINT MONEY.

VALLEY FORGE

IN DECEMBER, CONGRESS AND LOCAL BUSINESSMEN CONVINCE GEORGE "THE ROCK" WASHINGTON TO SET UP WINTER CAMP ON A BARE PLAIN OUTSIDE PHILADELPHIA. IT'S CALLED VALLEY FORGE.

CONGRESS REWARDS ITS HALF-STARVED SOLDIERS WITH A THANKSGIVING MEAL OF RICE AND VINEGAR...

... AS GENERAL HOWE PARTIES AWAY THE WINTER SOCIAL SEASON WITH THE TORY GENTRY.

THROUGH THE WINTER, WITH SUPPLIES ONLY TRICKLING IN, THE REBEL SOLDIERS ENDURE HUNGER AND DISEASE. THEY EAT FLOUR CAKES BAKED ON ROCKS AND THEY STAND GUARD IN BARE FEET.

I TOLD YOU! OFFICERS DO NOT FRATERNIZE WITH ENLISTED MEN!

B-BUT SIR, WE'RE JUST TRYING TO KEEP WARM.

CONGRESS IS PAYING THE TROOPS IN PROMISES. WITH FARMS AND FAMILIES BACK HOME, MANY SIMPLY LEAVE. THOSE WHO REMAIN ARE OFTEN THE POOR, THE AFRICANS, AND THE HOMELESS FOR WHOM THE MILITARY IS A COMFORT.

MEANWHILE, AMONG THE CIVILIANS, A NEW AGE IS DAWNING. BEFORE THE REBELLION, PEOPLE KEPT BUSY BEING ANGRY AT THE INTERFERING BRITISH OFFICIALS.

THE WAY IT WAS

IF WE WERE LEFT ALONE, THERE'D BE NO GREED AND WE'D CARE FOR OURSELVES AND EACH OTHER.

ROYAL CUSTOMS OFFICE

NOW, THOUGH THERE'S A WAR ON, PEOPLE ARE FREE TO LIVE IN HARMONY AND GOOD FELLOWSHIP...

YOU GET RID OF BIG GOVERNMENT AND TAXES AND THERE'LL BE NO MORE POOR PEOPLE.

PIG FOR SALE

BARGAIN

... AND FREE TO START BUSINESSES OF THEIR OWN.

IF THEY ARE FREE, WHITE, AND MALE, OF COURSE.

WITH A PIG, I CAN GO INTO THE BACON BUSINESS OR THE LEATHER SHOE BUSINESS.

PIG FOR BARGAIN

ONCE IN BUSINESS, MANY START DOING WHAT COMES NATURALLY TO BUSINESSPEOPLE — ESPECIALLY IN A WAR ECONOMY. THEY MARK UP EVERYTHING.

TOM PAINE SAYS PEOPLE ARE BASICALLY GOOD. SO WHATEVER I DO IS OKAY.

SHOES FOR SALE 6s. 7s. 8s.

ONE SIZE FITS ALL

PEOPLE WITH CONNECTIONS ARE BUSILY MONOPOLIZING, USING INSIDER INFORMATION, AND DOING BUSINESS WITH THE HIGHEST BIDDERS (WHICH MIGHT MEAN THE BRITISH OR THE FRENCH RATHER THAN THEIR OWN POOR COUNTRY).

AT THE SAME TIME, CONGRESS AND SOME STATES ARE PRINTING MORE AND MORE MONEY TO FINANCE THE WAR.

ENGLAND HAD NEVER ALLOWED HER COLONIES TO HAVE THEIR OWN MONEY.

NOW WE HAVE ALL WE WANT!

PAPER MONEY AND RISING PRICES BRING RUNAWAY INFLATION.

MEANWHILE, FOREIGN VOLUNTEERS ARE SHOWING UP ON CONGRESS' DOORSTEP LOOKING FOR MILITARY GLORY.

ONE VOLUNTEER IS BARON FRIEDRICH WILHELM AUGUSTUS VON STEUBEN. HE IMPRESSES GEORGE "THE ROCK."

GEORGE "THE ROCK" GIVES STEUBEN THE JOB OF TEACHING THE RAGGEDY TROOPS OF VALLEY FORGE THE BASICS OF TRADITIONAL SOLDIERING.

IN FEBRUARY, LOUIS XVI, AUTOCRATIC MONARCH OF FRANCE, SIGNS AN ALLIANCE WITH THE U.S. THE LITTLE REPUBLIC HAS NEW FINANCIAL AND MILITARY MUSCLE.

WITH THE COMING OF SPRING, "THE ROCK" HAS WON HIS BIGGEST BATTLE. THE MEN HAVE SURVIVED VALLEY FORGE, AND VON STEUBEN HAS TURNED THEM INTO A REAL ARMY.

106

But the army's new skills don't matter much because King George III has decided to move the war south.

The Tories and slaves in the South will join us. With their support we will end this foolishness.

TROUBLE AT HOME
SLAVERY

While England, the Continental Army, and Congress struggle through their war, there are other conflicts in the states. One is the slaves' battle against their oppressors.

SLAVES FOR SALE
PRIME HEALTHY

They retaliate through daily resistance and by escapes.

Our slaves keep running away, I don't know why. Have they no feelings for us?

Who will take care of us?

RUNAWAY SLAVES DISCOVER THAT THE BRITISH WILL USE THEM AS RIVER PILOTS, SPIES, HORSE TRAINERS, AND BOOTY, WHILE PROMISING FREEDOM. BUT FREEDOM REMAINS AN ELUSIVE DREAM.

AFTER WE'RE DONE WITH THE AFRICAN, WE'LL GIVE HIM TO SOME TORY.

UNOFFICIALLY, AFRICANS FOUGHT IN THE REBEL ARMY SINCE LEXINGTON. BUT BLACKS WITH GUNS TERRIFY AND ANGER MANY WHITES.

IF I FIND ANY OF MY RUNAWAYS IN UNIFORM, I'LL SUE THE ARMY AND HANG THE SLAVE.

BY LATE 1777, CONGRESS IS DESPERATE FOR SOLDIERS. THEY OFFER REWARDS TO STATES THAT PROVIDE SLAVES AND FREEDOM TO SLAVES WHO SERVE.

Hmmm

500 ACRES TO ANYONE WHO PROVIDES ONE STANDARD SIZE SLAVE.

RECRUITING OFFICE

FREEDOM TO ANY SLAVE WHO SERVES OUT HIS ENLISTMENT.

Hmmm

IN JULY OF 1778, THE UNITED STATES AND THEIR FRENCH ALLIES PLAN TO TAKE BACK NEWPORT, RHODE ISLAND. THERE'S A VIOLENT STORM AND DISAGREEMENTS BETWEEN THE REBEL AND FRENCH COMMANDERS. THE FRENCH FLEET SAILS AWAY FROM NEWPORT.

THE BRITISH ATTACK THE NOW ISOLATED, MOSTLY INEXPERIENCED U.S. MILITIAMEN. IN THE MIDDLE OF THE REBEL TROOPS IS AN AFRICAN REGIMENT FROM RHODE ISLAND.

THE AFRICAN REGIMENT HOLDS BACK THE ENGLISH AND GERMAN TROOPS WHILE...

ooo THE MARBLEHEAD FISHERMEN ONCE MORE SAVE THE DAY BY FERRYING THE U.S. TROOPS TO SAFETY. LATER, THE AFRICAN REGIMENT RECEIVES AN OFFICIAL COMMENDATION FOR BRAVERY.

AT THIS POINT MORE AND MORE AFRICANS ARE APPEARING IN THE MILITARY. THEY'RE FIGHTING FOR THE FLAG, BUT THEIR GOAL IS THEIR OWN FREEDOM.

WHEN NECESSARY, THE MILITARY CAN BE COLORBLIND. IN THE CIVILIAN WORLD, IT'S A DIFFERENT STORY:

A VIRGINIA SLAVE TRIES TO ESCAPE AND IS SENTENCED TO DEATH FOR TREASON. HIS OWNER WINS HIM BACK BY SAYING THAT PROPERTY CAN'T BE ACCUSED OF TREASON.

COURT HOUSE

In Boston, Paul Cuffe, an African shipowner, is taken to court for not paying his taxes. Cuffe says, since Africans can't vote they should not have to pay taxes. Cuffe loses.

THE AMERICAN INDIANS

During the war, bloody fighting raged up and down the frontier. Indians, allied with the Tories, fought the patriots. There were atrocities on both sides. But colonial propogandists used Indian cultural and martial differences to portray the Indians as mindless savages.

Meanwhile, the U.S. Army strips the flesh off dead Indians to make boots.

LATE IN 1779, WASHINGTON SENDS AN EXPEDITION TO ATTACK THE INDIANS OF WESTERN NEW YORK STATE. UNABLE TO MOUNT A DEFENSE, THE SMALLER INDIAN FORCES FADE INTO THE FOREST.

THE IROQUOIS CONFEDERACY IN THE NORTHEAST IS A SETTLED CULTURE OF TOWNS AND FARMS. IT HAS A CONSTITUTION, COUNCIL CENTERS, AND FRAME HOUSES WITH GLASS WINDOWS.

THE U.S. SOLDIERS COME ACROSS EMPTY INDIAN VILLAGES AND FARMS BURSTING WITH THE FALL HARVEST.

THE ARMY CONDUCTS A SCORCHED EARTH POLICY, DESTROYING THE VILLAGES AND FOOD FOR THE COMING WINTER. THEIR CAMPAIGN IS A VENGEFUL FAILURE.

GEORGE WASHINGTON'S NICKNAME AMONG THE INDIANS IS TOWN DESTROYER.

THE U.S. RAMPAGE ONLY INCREASES ATTACKS BY INDIANS ON FRONTIER VILLAGES. THEY ARE LED BY THE GREAT MOHAWK GENERAL, JOSEPH BRANT.

BRANT IS AN EDUCATED MAN (DARTMOUTH COLLEGE). HE LIVED IN ENGLAND AND RUBBED ELBOWS WITH BRITISH SOCIETY. HE COMES HOME TO FIGHT.

IN 1781, THE INDIANS ARE FINALLY AND LEGALLY DONE OUT OF THEIR LAND. THROUGH THE ARTICLES OF CONFEDERATION, CONGRESS CEDES ALL DISPUTED LAND TO ITSELF, THE NEW COUNTRY.

HE SAYS THAT THE MOUNTAINS NOW BELONG TO TOWN DESTROYER.

WOMEN

THEIR OPINIONS OFTEN BRUSHED ASIDE BY MEN, WOMEN ARE WAKING UP TO THE CONTRADICTIONS IN THEIR OWN LIVES. AND THEY EXPLORE IDEAS OF THEIR OWN REBELLION.

YET THEY ARE PATRIOTIC. WOMEN CONTRIBUTE TO THE WAR EFFORT AT HOME BY RAISING MONEY AND RUNNING THE FARMS AND BUSINESSES.

THEY ALSO LEAVE HOME TO RISK THEIR LIVES AS NURSES, SPIES, AND SECRET COURIERS.

AND SOME GO TO WAR DISGUISED AS MEN. IN THE AFTERMATH OF CARNAGE, THEIR DEAD BODIES ARE FOUND ON THE FIELD OF BATTLE.

ON ONE SIDE ARE THE POORER PEOPLE, THE "MORAL ECONOMISTS" WHO WANT PRICE CONTROLS.

NO ONE CARES ABOUT VIRTUE AND THE COMMON GOOD ANY MORE!

ON THE OTHER SIDE ARE THE "BUYER BEWARE" FREE MARKET ELITE WHO ARE MAKING BIG BUCKS.

THERE MUST BE NO RESTRAINT ON FREEDOM.

WAREHOUSE

IN THE CENTER IS THE NEW MIDDLE CLASS OF BUSINESSMEN. THEY'RE SIDING WITH THE RICH.

I'M OPENING A NEW SHOE STORE AND I DON'T WANT TO BE TOLD HOW MUCH TO CHARGE!

STANISLAW'S SHOES

STORE FOR RENT

BUT, WHILE THE FEAR OF REVOLT FROM WITHIN CENTERS ON THE AFRICANS, AMERICAN INDIANS, HUNGRY PEOPLE, AND ANGRY SOLDIERS, THE REAL VILLAIN AT HOME TURNS OUT TO BE...

OOO ONE OF WASHINGTON'S FAVORITE GENERALS, **B**ENEDICT **A**RNOLD. ARNOLD IS RECENTLY MARRIED TO THE DAUGHTER OF AN IMPORTANT TORY.

THEY LIVE LAVISHLY AND ARNOLD IS ALWAYS IN DEBT AND ON THE LOOKOUT FOR MONEYMAKING SCAMS.

ARNOLD IS ANGRY AT HIS COUNTRY FOR NOT REWARDING HIM WITH THE RANK, MONEY, AND GLORY HE THINKS HE DESERVES.

WEST POINT

ARNOLD CONVINCES "THE ROCK" TO GIVE HIM COMMAND OF WEST POINT. THE FORT AT WEST POINT GUARDS THE HUDSON RIVER NORTH OF NEW YORK CITY.

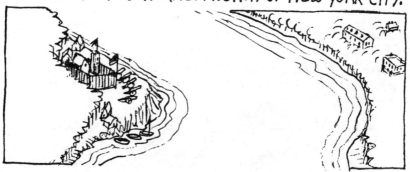

DURING THE WAR, GANGS OF THIEVES ROAM THE COUNTRYSIDE.

THEY PRETEND TO BE ROYALISTS OR PATRIOTS AS IT SUITS THEM.

WHICH SIDE SHOULD WE BE ON TODAY?

ONE NIGHT IN SEPTEMBER, 1780, IN THE WOODS NEAR WEST POINT, ONE OF THESE BANDS AMBUSHES A TRAVELER. IN HIS BOOT THEY FIND A MAP OF THE FORT.

THEY HAND OVER THE STRANGER TO THE MILITIA. HE'S REVEALED TO BE A BRITISH AGENT AND ARNOLD'S PLOT TO SURRENDER WEST POINT TO THE BRITISH IS UNCOVERED. BEFORE "THE ROCK" CAN ARREST HIM, ARNOLD ESCAPES TO THE BRITISH.

WHEN IT'S ALL SORTED OUT, WEST POINT IS SAVED, THE BRITISH AGENT IS HANGED, ARNOLD GETS MONEY AND A COMMISSION FROM BRITAIN, AND THE NEW COUNTRY HAS ITS FIRST INGLORIOUS **T**RAITOR !

BENEDICT ARNOLD

WAR IN THE SOUTH

IN 1780, THE GENERAL IN CHARGE OF THE SOUTHERN REBEL FORCES FOOLISHLY BARRICADES HIS ARMY IN CHARLES TOWN, SOUTH CAROLINA. HE'S ENCIRCLED BY THE BRITISH AND FORCED TO SURRENDER.

"**T**HE ROCK" APPOINTS GENERAL GATES, THE HERO OF SARATOGA (IN HIS OWN MIND) TO TAKE OVER A WEAKENED, DEMORALIZED SOUTHERN COMMAND.

GATES CHOOSES TO CONFRONT THE BRITISH IN SOUTH CAROLINA. THE BRITISH ALMOST DESTROY HIS ARMY. THE "HEROIC" GATES LEADS THE RETREAT.

CORNWALLIS, THE BRITISH LEADER, CONFIDENTLY MARCHES THROUGH THE SOUTH, RAIDING AND DESTROYING PROPERTY AND LIVES.

SEND A MESSAGE TO THE KING, "WE OWN THE SOUTH!"

BUT CORNWALLIS IS ANGERING THE ROUGH, TOUGH BACKCOUNTRY CIVILIANS. UP TILL NOW, THESE PEOPLE HAVE HATED THE RICH PLANTATION OWNERS FAR MORE THAN THE BRITISH. NO LONGER.

MA, GET ME M' RIFLE AND A BAG OF DRIED CORN. I'M OFF TO FIGHT THEM REDCOATS!

LED BY DANGEROUS MEN LIKE FRANCIS MARION, THE "SWAMP FOX," THESE SOUTHERN IRREGULARS STRIKE THE BRITISH AND DISAPPEAR INTO THE SWAMPS.

THEY WERE HERE A MINUTE AGO.

"THE ROCK" PICKS ONE OF HIS FAVORITE OFFICERS, RHODE ISLAND QUAKER-TURNED-SOLDIER NATHANAEL GREENE TO TAKE OVER FROM GATES.

NATE, YOU'RE YOUNG, MAYBE YOU HAVE SOME FRESH IDEAS.

GREENE TEAMS UP WITH THE "SWAMP FOX," AND BIG, OLD DANIEL MORGAN AND HIS RIFLEMEN. IN A CLEVER MOVE THEY SPLIT UP THEIR WEAK FORCES.

GUERRILLA TACTICS ARE WHAT WILL WORK HERE. WE WON'T TELL WASHINGTON.

THEY CONDUCT HIT-AND-RUN ATTACKS THAT CONFUSE CORNWALLIS. IN 1781, AT COWPENS IN SOUTH CAROLINA, MORGAN SETS UP HIS MEN IN AN IMAGINATIVE, UNORTHODOX FORMATION. HE LURES IN THE BRITISH, HITS THEM HARD, AND DISAPPEARS.

CORNWALLIS AND GREENE FINALLY MEET IN BATTLE AT GUILFORD COURT HOUSE. GREENE USES MORGAN'S PLOY. PART OF IT IS TO PUT HIS LESS-SKILLED MILITIA IN THE MIDDLE OF A FIELD. BEHIND THEM HE PLACES SHARPSHOOTERS WITH ORDERS TO SHOOT ANY MILITIA WHO DON'T STAND AND FIGHT.

GREENE BAITS HIS TRAP WITH MOUNTED IRREGULARS.

HEY, WE'RE OVER HERE.

THE PATRIOT ARMY KEEPS FIRING AND FALLING BACK, DRAWING THE BRITISH INTO A TRAP. THE BRITISH GAIN THE GROUND BUT SUFFER HEAVY LOSSES. GREENE RETREATS INTACT.

THE BATTERED CORNWALLIS LIMPS NORTH INTO VIRGINIA. GREENE AND HIS WILY OFFICERS, MARION, MORGAN, MAD ANTHONY WAYNE, AND LIGHT-HORSE HARRY LEE, LEADING A GROWING PEOPLE'S ARMY, ARE TAKING BACK THE SOUTH.

THOMAS JEFFERSON IS NOW THE GOVERNOR OF VIRGINIA. HE CONTINUES TO FIGHT FOR PROGRESSIVE CAUSES, CALLING FOR THE SEPARATION OF CHURCH AND STATE, FREE SCHOOLS, AND THE END OF SLAVERY.

THE PEN IS MIGHTIER THAN THE SWORD.

124

JEFFERSON ALSO BELIEVES ALL THE UGLY STEREOTYPES OF THE DAY: WOMEN AND AMERICAN INDIANS ARE NOT AS SMART AS WHITE MEN. AFRICANS ARE MORE MUSICAL, NEED LESS SLEEP, AND ARE MORE PASSIONATE LOVERS (BUT NOT SO TENDER).

SOMEDAY GOD WILL PUNISH US FOR SLAVERY. BUT FOR NOW, IT KEEPS ME OUT OF DEBT.

BUT JEFFERSON IS NOT MUCH OF A WAR GOVERNOR. AS THE BRITISH MARAUD THEIR WAY THROUGH VIRGINIA, TOM PLAYS HIS VIOLIN, DESIGNS BUILDINGS AND GARDENS, AND RECORDS THE HABITS OF FLORA AND FAUNA...

SIR, THE BRITISH ARE COMING!

NOT NOW. I'M STUDYING THE FLIGHT OF THE WILD GEESE.

SIR, THEY'RE ATTACKING RICHMOND!

CALL VON STEUBEN AND WASHINGTON!

SIR, THEY'RE COMING HERE TO MONTICELLO!

TELL MY SLAVES TO HIDE THE SILVERWARE! I'M LEAVING!

However, Cornwallis is under constant pressure from guerrilla bands. In August of 1781, he retires to Yorktown, Virginia, to lick his wounds. It's been six years of war and England is sick of it. Only King George III is for it.

Your Majesty, even if we kill all the men, the women and children will fight us. We can't win.

Fight harder! Change generals! It's Parliament's fault!

In New York, "The Rock's" army continues to shrink. He wants the French to join him for a major allied offensive in the north. Instead, the French head south to the Chesapeake Bay. "The Rock" has a stress attack.

Whose war is this, anyway? I'm supposed to be the commander here!

Then "The Rock" makes a momentous decision. He gathers his little army, the hardened survivors of years of fighting...

126

YORKTOWN

CORNWALLIS HAS BARRICADED HIMSELF IN YORKTOWN WITH THE BRITISH FLEET PROTECTING HIS REAR.

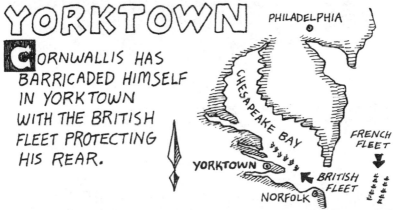

PHILADELPHIA

CHESAPEAKE BAY

FRENCH FLEET

YORKTOWN

BRITISH FLEET

NORFOLK

THE FRENCH FLEET SHOWS UP AND THERE'S A CONFUSING **N**AVAL **B**ATTLE.

TIREZ!
TACK!
AU SECOURS!

TURN TO PORT!
À GAUCHE!

OH LA LA
WHERE'S THE WIND?
WE'RE TAKING WATER! BAIL! BAIL!
WHERE'RE THE PADDLES?

WHEN THE SMOKE CLEARS, THE FRENCH CONTROL YORKTOWN HARBOR, AND CORNWALLIS IS CUT OFF. "THE ROCK" NOW HEADS A FORCE MADE UP OF 1/3 U.S. AND 2/3 FRENCH SOLDIERS. HE REALIZES THAT HERE IS THE CLASSIC BATTLE HE'S BEEN SEARCHING FOR FOR SIX YEARS.
I TOLD THEM, GUERRILLA WAR IS FOR GUERRILLAS.
"THE ROCK" IS FORGETTING ALL THE YEARS OF ACTION BY HIS PEOPLE'S ARMY THAT MADE THIS CONFRONTATION POSSIBLE.
SET UP SIEGE LINES...START THE ARTILLERY BOMBARDMENT... BUT FIRST, EVERYONE LINE UP FOR INSPECTION AND WIG POWDER!

THE UNIFIED ARMY RELEASES DEADLY MORTAR AND CANNON FIRE AGAINST A TRAPPED CORNWALLIS.

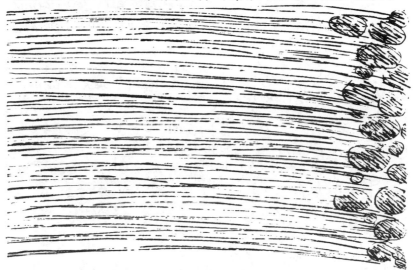

IN OCTOBER 1781, CORNWALLIS IS FORCED TO SURRENDER. THE DRAMATIC VICTORY DESTROYS ANY HOPE THE BRITISH HAVE OF HOLDING THEIR COLONIES.

IN THE STATES, GEORGE WASHINGTON IS THE BIG HERO. HIS OFFICERS, GREENE, LAFAYETTE, HAMILTON, ETC., ARE STARS. IN PARIS, FRANKLIN, JOHN JAY, AND JOHN ADAMS PLAY DIPLOMATIC GAMES WITH THE EUROPEAN POWERS.

ON SEPTEMBER 1783, A PEACE TREATY IS FINALLY SIGNED. ENGLAND'S FORMER COLONIES ARE OFFICIALLY A COUNTRY AND THE RADICAL LEADERS ARE IN CHARGE.

1782 - 1789

PROFIT & VIRTUE

THE CONFEDERATION

IT'S THE EARLY 1780s AND THE PEOPLE OF THE UNITED STATES ARE MOVING TOWARD THE FUTURE WITH COCKINESS AND NEW IDEAS. TRADERS VENTURE AS FAR AS CHINA. THE COTTON GIN, COAL AS FUEL, AND THE STEAM ENGINE ARE AROUND THE CORNER.

THEY SAY BOATS WILL SOON MOVE BY STEAM.

THAT'S A LOT OF HOT AIR! HAR, HAR!

THERE ARE ALL KINDS OF BREAKTHROUGHS.

IT'S CALLED COTTON. IT'S THE LATEST IN FASHION.

IT'S A BRUSH AND PASTE TO CLEAN TEETH.

WHAT'S WRONG WITH MY FINGER AND SNUFF?

MODERN MEDICINE NO LONGER PRESCRIBES COW DUNG POULTICES. NOW IT'S GARLIC AND DEER FAT.

AND EVERYONE IS INTO SELF-IMPROVEMENT!

I'M LATE FOR CLASS.

The New School

- IMPROVE YOUR MIND AND LOOKS
- CONQUER YOUR WEAKNESSES
- LEARN HOW MONEY BRINGS HAPPINESS

BUT PEOPLE ARE STILL FULL OF REGIONAL PRIDE AND SUSPICIOUS OF OUTSIDERS.

ONE THING I WON'T IMPROVE IS MY DISPOSITION!

ALONG WITH PROGRESS, THERE ARE SERIOUS MONEY PROBLEMS IN THE COUNTRY.

✔ THE MILITARY, WHOSE BACK-PAY CLAIMS ARE IGNORED BY CONGRESS, ARE THREATENING VIOLENCE.

UNFAIR TO VETS

HOW'D CONGRESS LIKE THE FEEL OF A BAYONET?

✔ FOREIGN GOODS ARE AGAIN POURING INTO THE COUNTRY, HURTING LOCAL MERCHANTS AND WORKERS.

✔ SETTLERS ARE FLOODING WEST IN THE NEW CONESTOGA WAGONS. BUT THERE'S CHAOS AS LAND COMPANIES, POLITICIANS, AND THE STATES JUMP ON THESE SQUATTERS' LAND CLAIMS.

✔ THE STATES ARE PRINTING PILES OF PAPER MONEY SO THEY CAN QUICKLY PAY OFF THEIR WAR DEBTS.

THE LEADER OF THE RICH AND POWERFUL IS ALEXANDER HAMILTON. RAISED BY A SINGLE MOM IN THE WEST INDIES, HAMILTON IMMIGRATES TO THE COLONIES SEEKING HIS FORTUNE. HE BECOMES A LAWYER, IS WASHINGTON'S AIDE DURING THE WAR, MARRIES BIG NEW YORK MONEY, AND GOES INTO POLITICS.

I SEE NATIONAL GREATNESS FOR THIS COUNTRY, AND IT IS MY DESTINY TO LEAD US TO GLORY.

ALEX CALLS THE COMMON PEOPLE "THE BEAST."

HAMILTON, WASHINGTON, JOHN ADAMS AND THE OTHERS WITH BIG STAKES IN THE GOVERNMENT DEBATE THE THREAT OF TROUBLE FROM THE MASSES.

ENOUGH OF THIS TALK OF GOVERNMENT FOR VIRTUE AND THE COMMON GOOD.

GOOD GOVERNMENT ENCOURAGES FOREIGN INVESTMENT, IT GUARDS AGAINST PAPER MONEY, AND IT PROTECTS US FROM UPRISINGS BY INDIANS, SLAVES, AND THE LOWER CLASSES.

139

140

THE POOR FARMERS ARE FAILING TO PAY FEED AND STOCK BILLS, THEY'RE DEFAULTING ON THEIR TAXES, AND THEIR FARMS ARE BEING CONFISCATED.

NEXT CASE!

UNDER NEW OWNERSHIP

BESSIE

THE FARMERS ARE THROWN INTO PRISON UNTIL THEY CAN PAY OFF THEIR BILLS.

B-BUT IF I'M IN JAIL, HOW CAN I PAY WHAT I OWE?

IT'S THE LAW!

MANY OF THE FARMERS, SITTING IN THEIR DANK CELLS, ARE REVOLUTIONARY WAR VETERANS.

THE RICH GO INTO DEBT, TOO. BUT THEY DON'T WORRY ABOUT PRISON.

I'LL PAY YOU WHAT I OWE YOU WITH A TIP ON A NEW BOND ISSUE.

141

THE FARMERS ARE BOILING MAD. THEY ORGANIZE MEETINGS, PREPARE GRIEVANCES, AND REQUEST HEARINGS. AT FIRST THEY'RE AGAINST MOB ACTION.

WE JUST WANT TO TELL OUR SIDE.

STATE OFFICES

BUT THE LEGISLATURE REFUSES TO FACE THE PROBLEM.

KNOCK KNOCK KNOCK

DO YOU HEAR ANYTHING?

NO

WHY?

AT THE CENTER OF THE TROUBLE ARE THE COURTS, WHERE LAWYERS HIRED BY CREDITORS PROSECUTE DEBTORS IN FRONT OF JUDGES.

IF WE CLOSE DOWN THE COURTS...

...THE STATE WILL HAVE TO PAY ATTENTION.

COUNTY COURTHOUSE

THE FARMERS DO WHAT WAS DONE IN THE EARLY DAYS OF THE REBELLION. THEY TAKE THEIR ANGER INTO THE STREETS.

USING THEIR BEST REVOLUTIONARY TECHNIQUES, THEY MOVE ON COURTHOUSES IN A NUMBER OF TOWNS.

JUDGES AND LAWYERS ARE QUICK TO GET THE IDEA.

WITH THE COURTS SHUT DOWN, CREDITORS CAN'T HURT THE FARMERS.

MORE AND MORE MASSACHUSETTS FARMERS ARE JOINING THE REBELLION. THE LEADER IS A LOCAL FARMER AND WAR VETERAN, DANIEL SHAYS.

TROUBLE IS BREWING IN OTHER STATES, TOO: TAX UPRISINGS IN RHODE ISLAND AND THE CAROLINAS, RENT STRIKES IN NEW YORK.

BUSINESSMEN AND POLITICIANS ARE HORRIFIED. THE MASSACHUSETTS MILITIA WON'T HELP BECAUSE THEY ARE IN SYMPATHY WITH THE FARMERS. AND CONGRESS HAS NO POWER TO ACT.

144

FINALLY, A PRIVATE ARMY IS RAISED BY BOSTON BUSINESSMEN AND SENT AFTER THE REBELS.

IF THOSE PEOPLE GET AWAY WITH THIS, OUR MONEY AND PROPERTY WILL NEVER BE SAFE.

BERKSHIRE MOUNTAINS

THE RURAL INSURGENTS DON'T HAVE THE SUPPORT OF THE CITY PEOPLE AND THE PRIVATE ARMY IS ABLE TO OVERCOME THEM.

I DIDN'T THINK IT WAS MY PROBLEM. I KNOW ABOUT SHOES, NOT COWS.

MAYBE IF WE'D HAD MORE LAWYERS ON OUR SIDE...

EVENTUALLY MOST OF THE REBELS ARE PARDONED, BUT "THE BETTER PEOPLE" ARE IN SHOCK.

EVERY TIME THEY HAVE A PROBLEM, THESE RIFFRAFF WILL REACH FOR THEIR PITCHFORKS.

THIS COULDN'T HAPPEN IN A MONARCHY.

EVEN A DICTATORSHIP WOULD BE OKAY IF IT KEPT AWAY TROUBLE AND CLEANED THE STREETS.

145

THOMAS JEFFERSON IS IN PARIS HOBNOBBING WITH THE FRENCH ARISTOCRACY.* HE WRITES A LETTER IN SUPPORT OF THE FARMERS.

"A LITTLE REBELLION IS A GOOD THING. THE TREE OF LIBERTY MUST BE REFRESHED WITH THE BLOOD OF PATRIOTS, AND TYRANTS... IT IS ITS NATURAL MANURE."

I THINK TOM'S HAD TOO MUCH FRENCH WINE.

* JEFFERSON AND JOHN ADAMS ARE IN EUROPE LOOKING FOR SUPPORT FOR THE NEW COUNTRY FROM THE NOW DISDAINFUL ENGLISH, FRENCH, AND SPANISH.

BUT MANY OF THE OLDER REBELS SOUND LIKE ROYALISTS.

SAM ADAMS:
THIS IS MOBISM CREATED BY TROUBLEMAKERS.

GEORGE WASHINGTON:
THIS MAKES US LOOK BAD. WHAT WILL EUROPE SAY?

JOHN ADAMS:
AN UNCHECKED DEMOCRACY IS... THE MOST DETESTABLE FORM OF GOVERNMENT.

THE ANGER AGAINST THE FARMERS' REBELLION IS WHAT MANY OF THE VERY IMPORTANT PEOPLE HAVE BEEN WAITING FOR.

WE NEED A CONSTITUTIONAL CONVENTION!

THESE "CONSTITUTIONALISTS" CALL FOR A MEETING OF THE STATES. THEY REASSURE THE NERVOUS "STATES RIGHTERS."

HEY, THIS IS JUST TO SUGGEST SOME MINOR CHANGES IN THE ARTICLES OF CONFEDERATION. NO BIG DEAL.

THE CONSTITUTIONALISTS ARE LED BY ALEXANDER HAMILTON, GEORGE "THE ROCK," AND JAMES MADISON, JR. SMALL, WISPY "JEMMY" MADISON IS FROM THE VIRGINIA ELITE. HE'S A PLANTATION OWNER, LAWYER, POLITICIAN, AND STUDENT OF GOVERNMENT.

BECAUSE PEOPLE ARE BASICALLY SELFISH, A GOVERNMENT MUST BE MADE OF CHECKS AND BALANCES.

JAMES MADISON

WHAT THESE IMPORTANT PEOPLE WANT IS PROTECTION. PROTECTION MEANS A GOVERNMENT WITH THE POWER TO TAX, TO KEEP A STANDING ARMY, TO DECLARE WAR, TO ENCOURAGE INTERNATIONAL TRADE...

... AND TO KEEP THE MASSES, WHO ARE USUALLY WRONG, FROM GETTING AT OUR MONEY.

THE CONSTITUTIONAL CONVENTION

IN 1787, 55 DELEGATES FROM EVERY STATE BUT RHODE ISLAND MEET IN PHILADELPHIA.

"ROGUE ISLAND," THE MOST ARGUMENTATIVE AND DEMOCRATIC OF THE STATES, IS CONTROLLED BY ITS AGRARIAN PARTY.

WE PREFER OUR OWN PAPER MONEY.

THE RICH, INFLUENTIAL, AND POWERFUL HAVE COME TO PHILADELPHIA TO ARGUE DEMOCRATIC PRINCIPLES.

A BIG, STRONG CENTRAL GOVERNMENT

BUSINESS WITHOUT INTERFERENCE

A SMALL GOVERNMENT AND RURAL ECONOMY.

The empire builders are there to create a new constitution.

The states' righters are there to defend against intrusive government.

A written constitution must come before any state or federal government.

Constitution? I thought we were here to discuss commerce!

The old radicals, Sam Adams and Patrick Henry, still promoting virtue and puritan values, stay home. A new generation is replacing them.

We smell a rat.

Pushed by the Madison-Hamilton crowd, "the rock" is elected president of the convention.

With Washington in there, the country will pay attention to us.

Immediately, the VIRGINIA RESOLVES are presented, and the delegates discover that they are discussing the fundamentals of government.

3 WHAT ABOUT SLAVERY? (THE CONSTITUTIONALISTS BADLY NEED THE SUPPORT OF THE SOUTH. THEY OFFER THE SOUTHERN DELEGATES A SWEETHEART DEAL.)

THE CONSERVATIVE DELEGATES REALIZE THEY ARE BEING OUTMANEUVERED BY THE PROPONENTS OF A STRONG CENTRAL GOVERNMENT.

THROUGH A SWELTERING SUMMER, STILL IN SECRET SESSION, THE DELEGATES BATTLE EVERY POINT.

FINALLY, IN THE FALL, THE DELEGATES EMERGE WITH A NEW CONSTITUTION OF SEVEN SHORT ARTICLES.

A PREAMBLE HAS BEEN WRITTEN BY THE VERY RICH AND SNOOTY GOVERNEUR MORRIS OF PENNSYLVANIA. HE INVENTS THE PHRASE, "WE THE PEOPLE..."

THE CONSTITUTION IS SIGNED BY A MAJORITY OF THE DELEGATES. THE OTHERS VOTE "NO" BY GOING HOME WITHOUT SIGNING.

A BILL OF RIGHTS HAD BEEN PROPOSED BUT VOTED DOWN BY THE CONVENTION.

THE CONSTITUTION IS SENT TO THE STATES FOR RATIFICATION. THE PEOPLE QUICKLY TAKE SIDES.

I LIKE IT. IT'S A WAY TO SOLVE OUR MONEY PROBLEMS.

I HATE IT! WE OVERTHREW AUTHORITY ONCE, AND NOW IT'S BACK AND IT'S <u>US</u>!

THE FRAMERS MADE THE PRINCIPLE OF THE POPULAR VOTE CENTRAL TO THE CONSTITUTION, BUT THEY ALSO KEPT THE MAJORITY AT A DISTANCE.

IT SAYS THAT THOSE WHO HAVE THE RIGHT TO VOTE WILL VOTE "INDIRECTLY" FOR PRESIDENT AND SENATORS. THE PRESIDENT WILL APPOINT THE SUPREME COURT.

THE ONLY DIRECT VOTE WILL BE FOR THE HOUSE OF REPRESENTATIVES.

THE MAIN CRITERIA FOR VOTING WILL BE: WHITE, MALE, AND PROPERTY OWNER.

I FOUGHT IN THE WAR, AND NOW THEY THINK I CAN'T VOTE BY PUTTING A KERNEL OF CORN IN A HAT UNLESS I OWN PROPERTY!

154

155

THE PEOPLE WHO ARE AGAINST THE CONSTITUTION ARE CALLED ANTI-FEDERALISTS.

THE ONLY GOVERNABLE COUNTRY IS SMALL, HOMOGENEOUS, STATE-DOMINATED, RURAL, AND RUN ON PURITAN PRINCIPLES.

A BIG CENTRAL GOVERNMENT IS FULL OF LAZY BUREAUCRATS DOING THE DEVIL'S WORK.

THE PEOPLE WHO ARE FOR THE CONSTITUTION ARE CALLED FEDERALISTS. JAMES MADISON SPEAKS FOR THEM.

BIG AND DIVERSE AREN'T BAD, THEY'RE GOOD. REGIONAL, CULTURAL, AND RACIAL DIFFERENCES WILL HELP EVERYONE. THE MORE DISAGREEMENTS AMONG PEOPLE, THE HARDER IT WILL BE TO FORM A MAJORITY.

THE EMERGING URBAN MIDDLE CLASS OF ARTISANS, CRAFTSMEN, AND SMALL BUSINESS PEOPLE ARE A SWING VOTE. THESE ENTREPRENEURS DECIDE THEY HAVE MORE IN COMMON WITH THE BIG BUSINESS FEDERALISTS.

FROM 1787 TO 1789, WITH THE FEDERALISTS PUSHING HARD, STATE AFTER STATE PASSES THE CONSTITUTION, AND SO IT IS ADOPTED. (IN 1790, RHODE ISLAND IS THE LAST STATE TO RATIFY.)

WHAT WAS I GOING TO DO? BE MY OWN COUNTRY.?

THE COUNTRY CELEBRATES THE NEW CONSTITUTION WITH HUGE PARADES.

THERE ARE FLOATS, BANDS, FLAGS, AND CANNONS. POLITICIANS, THE MILITARY, THE CLERGY, PROFESSORS, DOCTORS, AND BIG MERCHANTS PROUDLY STEP FORWARD. BUT THE BULK OF THE MARCHERS ARE THE NEW MIDDLE CLASS TRADES AND CRAFTS WORKERS MARCHING IN THEIR OWN SPECIAL GROUPS *

* BAKERS, BLACKSMITHS, BOAT BUILDERS, BREWERS, BRICK MAKERS, CANDLE MAKERS, CARPENTERS, CATERERS, CLOCK MAKERS, COACH MAKERS, COOPERS, GOLDSMITHS, GUNSMITHS, PRINTERS, ROPE MAKERS, SADDLE MAKERS, SHOEMAKERS, SUGAR REFINERS, TAILORS, TOBACCONISTS, TOOL MAKERS, WHEELWRIGHTS...

THE REVOLUTIONARY ERA HAS NOW COME TO AN END. A GROUP OF EDUCATED, AMBITIOUS MEN HAS AROUSED A CITIZENRY WITH THE IDEAL OF EQUAL RIGHTS FOR ALL AND LED THEM TO VICTORY. TOGETHER THEY CREATE A STRONG REPUBLICAN GOVERNMENT WITH AN AGGRESSIVE MARKET ECONOMY.

AND THE FARMERS WILL HAVE TO ADAPT TO THE NEW ECONOMIC REALITIES.

HOME BREWED ★ IS BEST ★

GEORGE WASHINGTON IS ELECTED THE FIRST PRESIDENT. JOHN ADAMS, THOMAS JEFFERSON, AND JAMES MADISON WILL SUCCEED HIM AS PRESIDENT. ALEXANDER HAMILTON IS THE FIRST SECRETARY OF THE TREASURY. (HE'S KILLED IN A DUEL IN 1804.)

MAD JAMES OTIS DIED IN 1783 WHEN THE HOUSE HE WAS IN WAS HIT BY LIGHTNING

PATRICK HENRY LEADS THE FIGHT FOR A BILL OF RIGHTS. HE VOTES AGAINST THE CONSTITUTION AND BECOMES A SUCCESSFUL CRIMINAL LAWYER.

I'VE HAD IT WITH POLITICS!

P. HENRY ATTORNEY AT LAW

SAM ADAMS VOTES FOR THE CONSTITUTION. POORER AT THE END OF THE WAR THAN AT THE BEGINNING, HE RETURNS TO BOSTON POLITICS.

THEY HAVE STRAYED FROM THE PATH OF PIETY.

TOM PAINE IS NEVER ACCEPTED AS A TRUE FOUNDING FATHER. HE JOINS A POPULAR UPRISING IN ENGLAND AND THE REVOLUTION IN FRANCE. BUT HE COMES BACK TO HIS ADOPTED COUNTRY, THE U.S., TO DIE (1809).

TOM PAINE JUST DIED.

WHO?

THE BILL OF RIGHTS

THE BILL OF RIGHTS IS WRITTEN BY JAMES MADISON AND PASSED BY THE FIRST CONGRESS. IT BECOMES THE FIRST TEN AMENDMENTS TO THE CONSTITUTION. IT IS WHAT MOST PEOPLE THOUGHT THEY WERE FIGHTING FOR IN THE FIRST PLACE.

THE BILL OF RIGHTS HAS BECOME A SYMBOL OF INDIVIDUAL FREEDOMS. WHOEVER YOU ARE, IF YOU ARE HARMED OR DISCRIMINATED AGAINST BY ANY CROWD OR GROUP, YOU HAVE THE SAME RIGHT TO JUSTICE AS ANYONE ELSE.

163

THOUGH THOSE IN POWER HAVE CONTINUOUSLY REINTERPRETED THE CONSTITUTION, IN PRINCIPLE, ANYONE IN THIS SOCIETY IS AS GOOD AS ANYONE ELSE.

THERE ARE LOTS OF THINGS LEFT UNSETTLED BY THE CONSTITUTION. ★ SLAVERY CONTINUES. FREE AFRICANS HAVE FEW FREEDOMS. ★ THE DESTRUCTION OF THE NATIVE CULTURES PROCEEDS. ★ WHITES WITHOUT PROPERTY DO NOT HAVE AN EQUAL SHARE IN THEIR COUNTRY. ★ WOMEN HAVE NO MORE RIGHTS THAN BEFORE THE WAR.

BUT ALL THESE DISENFRANCHISED PEOPLE NOW UNDERSTAND THE IDEAS OF EQUALITY AND DISSENT. AND THEY WILL PASS ON THESE THOUGHTS TO THEIR SONS AND DAUGHTERS.

AND WHAT OF IDEALS LIKE LIVING IN HARMONY, WORKING FOR THE COMMON GOOD, CIVIC FAIRNESS, AND HONEST LABOR, WHICH THE PEOPLE ALSO FOUGHT FOR? THEY WILL BE TAUGHT TO CHILDREN, THEY WILL LIVE ON AS SLOGANS, THEY WILL FUEL MOVEMENTS TOWARD A GENUINE DEMOCRACY, AND THEY WILL BE PROCLAIMED IN POLITICAL CAMPAIGNS.